playful
Precut Quilts

15 Proje
with Block

C000226253

Amanda Niederhauser

stash BOOKS.
an imprint of C&T Publishing

Text copyright © 2020 by Amanda Niederhauser

Photography and artwork copyright © 2020 by C&T Publishing, Inc.

Publisher: Amy Barrett-Daffin

Creative Director: Gailen Runge

Acquisitions Editor: Roxane Cerda

Managing Editor: Liz Aneloski

Editor: Beth Baumgartel

Technical Editor: Linda Johnson

Cover/Book Designer: April Mostek

Production Coordinator: Zinnia Heinzmann

Production Editor: Jennifer Warren

Illustrator: Kirstie L. Pettersen

Photo Assistants: Gregory Ligman and Kaeley Hammond

Photography by Estefany Gonzalez of C&T Publishing, Inc., unless otherwise noted

Published by Stash Books, an imprint of C&T Publishing, Inc., P.O. Box 1456, Lafayette, CA 94549

Library of Congress Cataloging-in-Publication Data

Names: Niederhauser, Amanda, 1974- author.

Title: Playful precut quilts : 15 projects with blocks to mix & match / Amanda Niederhauser.

Description: Lafayette, CA : Stash Books, [2020]

Identifiers: LCCN 2019058646 | ISBN 9781617459498 (trade paperback) | ISBN 9781617459504 (ebook)

Subjects: LCSH: Patchwork--Patterns. | Quilting--Patterns.

Classification: LCC TT835 .N495 2020 | DDC 746.46/041--dc23

LC record available at https://lccn.loc.gov/2019058646

Printed in the USA

10 9 8 7 6 5 4 3 2

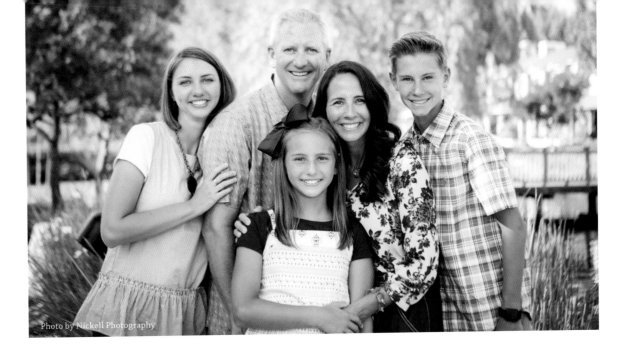

Photo by Nickell Photography

Dedication

To David, the love of my life, who has never complained about late-night sewing marathons, stepping on pins in the carpet, or the house being disastrous because I was too busy sewing. Thank you for letting me be me.

To my children, Ella, Ryan, and Sally: You are my everything. Thank you for being understanding when you leave the house covered in thread, when you have to hold quilts for photographs, and when I forget to pick you up from school because I'm sewing.

To Mufasa, the best cat in the whole world. You've been by my side every step of the way. Actually, you've been *in* my way: on the cutting mat, on my sewing chair, and on the quilt I've just basted!

To my quilty Instagram friends, thank you for supporting, encouraging, and humoring me.

To Jesus, the source of my strength and who I can do all things through.

To God, the ultimate creator, the giver of all good gifts, and the source of my inspiration.

Acknowledgments

A special thanks to Riley Blake Designs: You took a chance on me years ago, and I have loved our relationship. Thank you for letting me work with your amazing fabric.

Thanks to Moda Fabrics + Supplies and Cotton + Steel for allowing me to sew with your fabrics.

Thank you to Hobbs Bonded Fibers for graciously letting me use your batting in my quilts.

Thank you to my sweet friend Kaylene Parry, who quilted each of my quilts.

To my friend Tina, who believed in me when I didn't believe in myself.

Finally, thank you to C&T Publishing for supporting me and bringing my quilts to life.

Contents

projects 20

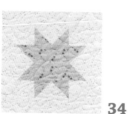

22

28

34

40

46

54

60

68

74

78

84

92

98

102

106

introduction

My quilt journey began twenty years ago when I attended a women's church activity. We were each to make a small wallhanging that included a center theme fabric with several border strips. While I was sewing my borders, the woman in charge exclaimed, "Ladies, your ¼″ seams look fabulous!" I looked down at my seams only to realize they were far from fabulous—more like disastrous! She was not talking about me. I could have been easily discouraged by this experience and vowed to never quilt again. Instead, I felt an awakening inside myself and wanted more. I purchased quilting books (because YouTube wasn't invented yet) and lots of fabric. I made quilt after quilt, making every mistake along the way but also learning a great deal in the process. I became excited by the creative process and began to dream in quilt designs!

Playful Precut Quilts is my way of sharing the creative process with you! I've created fifteen quilts based on 12″ blocks that give you the opportunity to add your personality, customize for any occasion, and let you mix and match blocks and settings. Each project in this book is made with 12″ blocks, and you can swap any of them! Each block is versatile because a variety of fabrics suits all the patterns. My sincere desire is that this becomes your go-to book when you want to make a table runner for your friend's birthday, a baby quilt for your newborn niece, or a throw quilt for your parent's anniversary.

Quilting brings me joy, and I hope it brings you joy as well. Wherever you are on your quilt journey—whether this is your first quilting experience or you've been quilting for 40 years—embrace the creative process! Let your personality shine through in what you make.

Fabric Precuts, Backing, and Batting

Precuts—A Quilter's Best Friend

I find myself shopping at quilt shops most often when I don't have a specific project in mind. I go to be inspired, to see what's new, or because I'm on vacation. It's often difficult to decide what to buy so I gravitate toward precuts. I can coordinate a stack of fat quarters in a snap or grab a precut bundle of 5˝ squares. I always make sure to choose coordinating yardage for a border or binding. If a pattern calls for precut squares or strips, you can always cut them from yardage yourself.

Quilting fabrics usually measure about 42˝ wide. All measurements in this book are based on 40˝-wide fabric to make sure that you have enough since fabric widths do vary. Width of fabric is abbreviated as *WOF*.

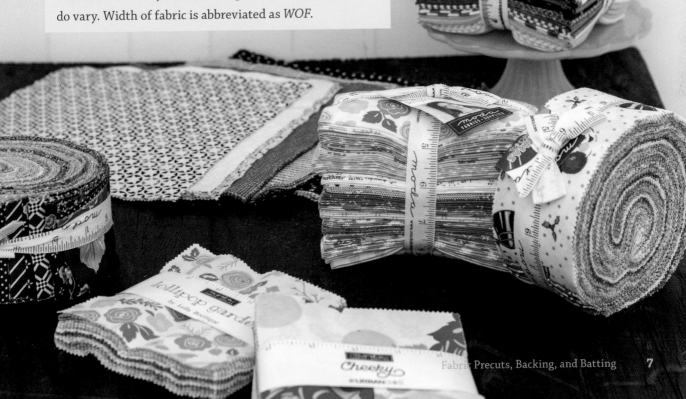

5″ Precut Squares

Bundles of 5″ squares, often called *charm packs* or *5″ Stackers*, are a brilliant invention. Within each bundle are a wide variety of fabrics, usually within a specific fabric line. You get a little taste of each fabric without having to purchase yardage.

2½″-Wide Precut Strips

Another handy invention
is the precut strip bundle.
These strips are some-
times referred to as *Jelly
Rolls* or *Rolie Polies*. They
measure 2½″ × WOF, which is
about 42″. These are great for
strip piecing and Log Cabin–
style quilts, and they can be
cut to a wide range of sizes.

10″ Precut Squares

Bundles of 10″ squares, often called *Layer Cakes* or *10″ Stackers*, have the same variety as 5″ bundles only they are larger. These larger pieces allow for even more versatility. They can be cut into quarters to equal 4 squares 5″ × 5″, cut into 2½″ strips, or cut evenly into 2½″ squares.

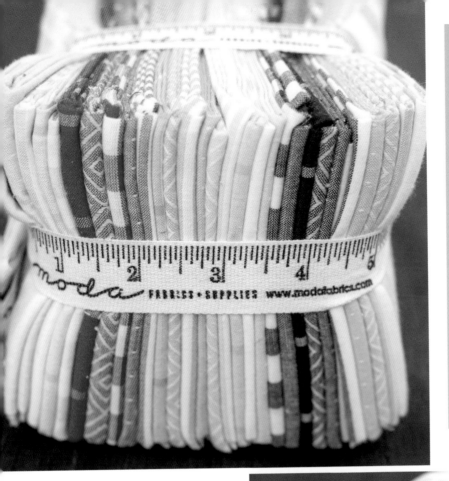

Fat Quarters

Because a wider piece of fabric is often better than a skinny piece of fabric, quilters invented the fat quarter. A fat quarter measures 18″ × 22″. It's still a ¼ yard of fabric, just the fat way! Quilt shops often cut them upon request. They are a great way to add to your stash when you're not sure what you are going to make. You can always cut them down to 5″ squares, 10″ squares, or 2½″ strips as a pattern requires. In this book, the width of a fat quarter is considered 21″ and is abbreviated *WOFQ*.

Fat Eighths

Fat eighths are just like fat quarters, only they are an ⅛ yard of fabric measuring 9″ × 22″. You'd be surprised what you can make with these little babies!

TIP: SCRAPS I used to store all my scraps in a box and then never open the box. (Who wants to dig through a random, wrinkly mess?) If you cut your scraps into precut sizes, you'll be more likely to use them and not waste them. Because so many quilt patterns call for precuts, cut remnants of fabric into 5″ or 10″ squares or 2½″ strips. This makes using scraps so easy.

fabric volume

When talking about fabric, *low volume* and *high volume* refer to the pattern or design and how it reads when mixed with other fabrics. Several projects in this book suggest purchasing either low-volume fabric or high-volume fabric to achieve the look of the featured quilt.

Low-Volume Fabric

Low-volume fabric pops up often in the quilting community and refers to fabric that is in the cream/white/neutral family. The fabric may have a small design or print but it reads neutral. If you're not sure if your fabric is low volume, place it with the fabrics you are considering and take a step back to look. From a distance it should look neutral.

High-Volume Fabric

High-volume fabric is the opposite of low-volume fabric; these fabrics are full of color and can be solid or patterned.

Backing

There are several choices of fabric when it comes to quilt backing. Most often I use quilting cotton that coordinates with my quilt top. You can also piece quilting fabric together in large sections, add an accent row, or even quilt blocks to your quilt back. If I know the quilt is going to be a "snuggle on the couch" quilt, I put minky on the back. We have a stack of quilts in the family room with minky backs, and they are our favorites! Flannel is another good choice for a soft and cozy back—just make sure you prewash and dry the flannel before using it to ensure that it doesn't shrink before quilting. One last quilt back option is to use a high-quality cotton bedsheet. I used a vintage sheet on the back of one quilt. So cute!

Preparing the Backing

Plan on cutting or making the quilt backing at least 8″ longer and 8″ wider than the quilt top. Most often this will involve piecing the fabric.

Here is my quick formula to decide how much fabric you will need.

If the quilt top is between 34″ and 74″ in length:

1. Add 8″ to the width of the quilt top, divide this number by 36, and then multiply it by 2. This number indicates the total yardage needed.

2. Cut the yardage in half widthwise. Sew the 2 pieces right sides together using a ½″ seam along the selvages. Trim the seam down to ¼″.

If the quilt top is longer than 74″ in length:

1. Add 8″ to the width of the quilt top, divide this number by 36, and then multiply it by 3. This number indicates total yardage needed.

2. Cut the yardage widthwise in 3 equal lengths (in thirds). Sew the selvages right sides together using a ½″ seam to create one piece of fabric with 3 equal-size sections. Trim the seams down to ¼″.

Batting

Typically batting is sold in widths wide enough that you don't have to piece the batting, like you do the backing fabric. Most battings are 60″, 96″, or 120″ wide.

The variety of battings available is simply amazing. It can almost be overwhelming. I have narrowed my batting preference down to the following two types.

• Heirloom Premium 80/20 Cotton/Poly Blend (by Hobbs Bonded Fibers) offers more loft and less weight than traditional cotton batting. It is durable and machine washable. This batting is made with a blend of 80% natural cotton and 20% fine polyester, is needle punched, and has a light resin bonding to provide exceptional strength and durability. Close quilting yields a flat, low-loft appearance, while more space between stitching lines yields a slightly higher loft.

• I also use Heirloom Premium 100% Natural Cotton with Scrim (by Hobbs Bonded Fibers). It is soft and pliable, made with high-grade cotton, and combined with a very thin polyester scrim (stabilizer) that is needle punched into the cotton fibers. This scrim adds superior strength to the cotton, and prevents the cotton batting from stretching and distorting as it's manipulated.

TIP If you quilt a lot, you end up with a stack of batting scraps. Don't throw them away! You can piece batting together. Make sure the edges of the batting are cut straight and are not crooked. Then, using a large zigzag stitch, push the edges of the batting together and zigzag stitch so the stitch catches both pieces of batting. This allows the batting to lie flat, and the quilting reinforces the batting seam.

Quilting Basics

Before you begin your quilt, make sure to read these basic quilting guidelines and techniques.

Seam Allowances

¼″ seam allowances are used for most projects. It's a good idea to stitch a test seam before you begin sewing to check that your machine stitches an accurate ¼″-wide seam. Accuracy is the key to successful piecing.

Stitching Seams

There is no need to backstitch at the beginning and end of most seams. Seamlines are usually crossed by another seam, which anchors the stitches.

Pressing

Press all seams in the direction indicated by the arrows in the diagrams or written in the instructions. Seams are either pressed to one side or pressed open. It's easier to press seams open by pressing them first to one side and then open. Use an up-and-down motion (not back-and-forth) to avoid distorting the fabric. Be especially careful when pressing bias edges, as they stretch easily.

Right Sides Together (RST)

The seams in this book are sewn *right sides together*. This means the printed sides of the fabric, or the right sides of the fabric, are facing each other. Right sides together can be abbreviated as *RST*.

Half-Square Triangles (HST)

Half-square triangles are featured frequently throughout this book. They are used to create different geometric patterns and are very simple to make. There are two ways to make them. One method produces two half-square triangles that need to be squared up after pressing; the other method produces one half-square triangle, but it doesn't need to be squared up.

Making Two Half-Square Triangles

Sew ¼″ away from both sides of the diagonal line to yield 2 half-square triangles.

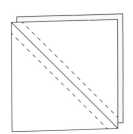

1. Start with 2 same-size, different-color squares.

2. Draw a diagonal line on the wrong side of one square.

3. Place the 2 squares RST and sew ¼″ away from both sides of the diagonal line.

4. Cut on the diagonal line, yielding 2 HSTs. Press open.

5. Square up each HST to the desired size.

 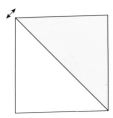

Making One Half-Square Triangle

Sew on the diagonal line to yield 1 half-square triangle.

1. Draw a diagonal line on the wrong side of one square.

2. Place 2 same-size, different-color squares RST.

3. Sew directly on the diagonal line.

4. Trim the seam allowance to ¼″.

5. Press the seam open. Discard the scraps.

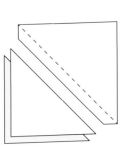 

  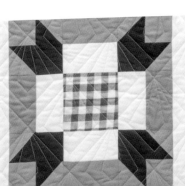 

Finishing

Instructions for basting, quilting, and binding are provided below.

Layering

Spread the pressed backing wrong side up and tape the edges to a flat surface with masking tape. (If you are working on carpet, you can use T-pins to secure the backing to the carpet.) Center the batting on top, smoothing out any folds. Place the quilt top right side up on top of the batting and backing, making sure it is centered. This is often referred to as the *quilt sandwich*.

Basting

Basting keeps the quilt sandwich layers from shifting while you are quilting.

If you plan to machine quilt, *pin baste* the quilt layers together with safety pins placed about 3″–4″ apart. Begin placing the pins in the center and move toward the edges, first in vertical and then horizontal rows. Try not to pin directly on the intended quilting lines.

As an alternative to pinning, try using a basting spray (like SpraynBond) to hold the layers together. The spray is temporary and washes out. It holds all the layers of the quilt sandwich together without pins. Spray the wrong side of the quilt back and lay the batting on top, smoothing any wrinkles. Then spray the batting and lay the quilt top on top, smoothing the wrinkles.

Quilting

Quilting, whether by hand or machine, enhances the pieced or appliquéd design of the quilt. You may choose to quilt-in-the-ditch, echo the pieced designs, use patterns from quilting design books and stencils, or do your own free-motion quilting.

Binding the Quilt

The binding for all projects in this book is 2½″ wide.

1. Prepare the binding by sewing 2½″ strips together using diagonal seams until you reach the necessary length. **FIG. A**

2. Trim the seam allowances and press the seams open to reduce bulk. Press the binding in half lengthwise, wrong sides together.

3. Starting in the middle of one side of the quilt, line up the raw edges of the binding with the raw edge of the quilt. Skipping the first 8″ of the binding, use a ¼″ seam allowance to stitch the binding to the quilt. Stop ¼″ away from the first corner and backstitch 1 stitch. **FIG. B**

4. Lift the presser foot and needle. Rotate the quilt one-quarter turn. Fold the binding at a right angle so it extends straight above the quilt and the fold forms a 45° angle in the corner. **FIG. C**

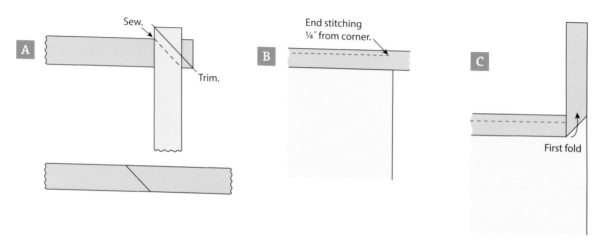

A — Sew. Trim.

B — End stitching ¼″ from corner.

C — First fold

5. Bring the binding strip down even with the edge of the quilt. Begin sewing at the folded edge. Repeat in the same manner at all corners. FIG. D

6. Once you have pivoted at all corners, keep sewing until you have 12″ left to reach the beginning stitches. Trim the tails of each end of the binding to overlap by exactly 2½″. Unfold the binding tails and bring them right sides together, matching the edges, as shown. Mark a diagonal

line as indicated. Sew along the marked line, trim the ¼″ seam, and press the seam open. FIG. E

7. Fold the binding back in half and pin in place onto the quilt top (it should be an exact fit). You can give it a little press with the iron to make it lie nicely. Finish stitching the binding in place.

8. Bring the folded edge of the binding up and over to the back of the quilt. Pin in place and miter the corners. Hand stitch the binding in place.

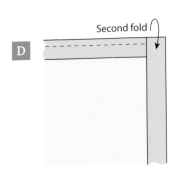

D

Second fold

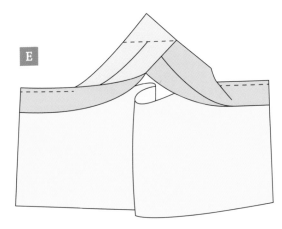

E

projects

garden cat

I have fond memories of my mother spending summer afternoons in the garden. I could always find her in her garden gloves and sun hat, kneeling down and carefully trimming and weeding her flowers. Cats often found refuge from the hot sun amidst the bushes of English sweet peas. There were always cats in our garden—some were pets, and some came around because of the fresh catnip and cat grass growing. Cats and gardens just seem to go together! Those sunny summer scenes of beautiful flowers and the cats that called our garden home inspired this quilt.

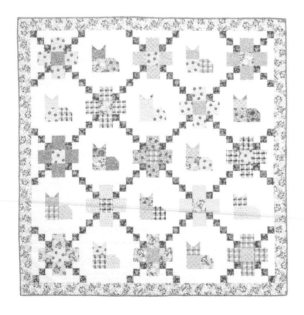

materials

The wide variety of prints found in a precut pack will give this quilt a scrappy feel.

5″ PRECUT SQUARES: 3 packs for blocks (113 high-volume squares in blues, greens, and pinks are required. Use 4 packs if the fabric collection is comprised of less than 90% high-volume prints.)

WHITE SOLID: 3¼ yards for background

RED FLORAL: 1½ yards (¾ yard for four-patches and cornerstones, ¾ yard for binding)

WHITE FLORAL: 1 yard for outer border

BACKING: 5 yards

BATTING: 87″ × 87″

Pieced by Amanda Niederhauser,
quilted by Kaylene Parry

Fabrics: May Belle collection by Jodi Nelson of Pleasant Home
for Penny Rose Fabrics (Riley Blake Designs)

cutting

5″ precut squares

- Set aside 13 sets of 4 identical squares for the Garden Path blocks. Doing this first will assure that 13 complete sets are on hand when needed. Separate the remaining precuts into color piles of blue, green, and pink.

White solid

Garden Path blocks

- Cut 7 strips 2½″ × WOF for the four-patches.

Cat blocks

- Cut 1 strip 12½″ × WOF and 2 strips 2½″ × WOF. Subcut into 24 rectangles 12½″ × 2½″ for the block frames.

- Cut 1 strip 8½″ × WOF and 2 strips 2½″ × WOF. Subcut into 24 rectangles 8½″ × 2½″ for the block frames.

- Cut 2 strips 4½″ × WOF. Subcut into:

  12 squares 4½″ × 4½″ for the cat background

  12 rectangles 4½″ × 2″ for the ear unit

- Cut 1 strip 2″ × WOF. Subcut into 12 squares 2″ × 2″ for the body unit.

Sashing

- Cut 4 strips 12½″ × WOF. Subcut into 60 rectangles 12½″ × 2½″.

Red floral

- Cut 19 strips 2½″ × WOF.

  Subcut 3 strips into 36 squares 2½″ × 2½″ for the sashing cornerstones.

  Set aside 7 strips for the Garden Path block four-patches.

  Set aside 9 strips for the binding.

White floral

- Cut 8 strips 4″ × WOF for the border.

Making the Cat Block

All seams are ¼″ unless otherwise noted. Follow the pressing arrows shown in the illustrations.

1. Choose 4 assorted 5″ squares from one color pile.

- From 1 square, cut 2 squares 2″ × 2″ for the ears.

- From 1 square, cut 1 rectangle 4½″ × 3″ for the face.

- Trim 2 squares to 4½″ × 4½″ for the body.

2. Draw a diagonal line on the wrong side of the 2″ cat-ear squares.

3. Position the squares at each end of a white background rectangle 4½″ × 2″, RST. Sew on the diagonal lines. Trim off the corners, leaving a ¼″ seam allowance. Press toward the ears. This creates the ear unit. **FIG. A**

4. Sew the ear unit to the face rectangle 4½″ × 3″. Press toward the face unit. Sew a 4½″ white background square to the right side of the face/ear unit, RST. This creates the head unit.

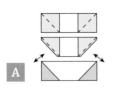

A

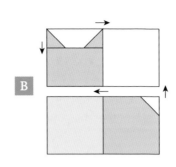

B

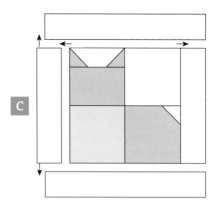

C

5. Sew 2 body squares together side by side; press toward the square on the left to create a horizontal body unit.

6. Draw a diagonal line on the wrong side of a 2″ white background square. Position it RST on the top right corner of the body unit. Sew on the diagonal line and trim off the corners, leaving a ¼″ seam allowance. Press toward the background.

7. Sew the head unit to the body unit, matching the center seams. Press toward the head unit. FIG. B

8. Add the block frame by sewing a white background rectangle 8½″ × 2½″ to each side of the Cat block. Press toward the background rectangles.

9. Sew a white background rectangle 12½″ × 2½″ to the top and bottom of the Cat block to complete the frame. Press toward the background rectangles. Make 12 Cat blocks. FIG. C

Making the Garden Path Block

1. Select 1 set of 4 identical precut squares (previously set aside) and 1 accent square. Trim each to 4½″ × 4½″.

2. Make a strip set using 1 white background strip and 1 red floral strip 2½″ × WOF. Sew these RST lengthwise. Press toward the red. Make 7 strip sets.

3. Cut the strip sets into 2½″-wide units (16 per set; 104 are used). FIG. D

4. Sew 2 units RST to form a four-patch, matching the center seam intersections. Press toward one side. Make 52 four-patches. FIG. E

5. Lay out the quilt block. Sew the 4½″ squares and four-patches together in rows and press, following the arrows. Sew the rows together, matching at each seam intersection. Press toward the center. Make 13 Garden Path blocks. FIG. F

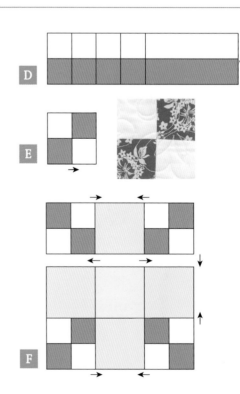

D

E

F

Assembling the Quilt

1. To make a sashing row, sew 6 red 2½″ cornerstones in between and at each end of 5 white 12½″ sashing rectangles. Sew the rectangles and squares together. Make 6 sashing rows.

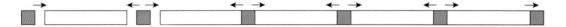

2. To make a block row, sew a white sashing rectangle 12½″ × 2½″ in between and at each end of 5 blocks. Make 5 block rows.

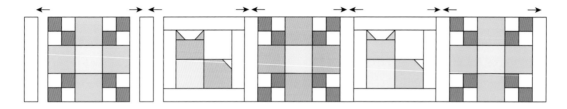

3. Lay out the quilt according to the quilt assembly diagram, alternating the sashing rows and block rows.

4. Sew the quilt together. Press toward the sashing rows.

TIP I like to press each row as I sew it to the next instead of pressing the whole quilt at the end. This reduces bulk when pressing and I love having only one seam to press at the end!

5. Piece the 8 border strips end to end. Subcut into 2 side borders 4″ × 72½″ and 2 top and bottom borders 4″ × 79½″.

6. Sew the side borders to the quilt front. Press toward the border.

7. Sew the top and bottom borders to the quilt front. Press toward the border.

Finishing

For more details, see Finishing (page 16).

1. Baste the quilt backing, batting, and quilt top together. Hand or machine quilt as desired. This quilt was machine quilted with a Sweat Pea design.

2. Make the binding and attach it to the quilt.

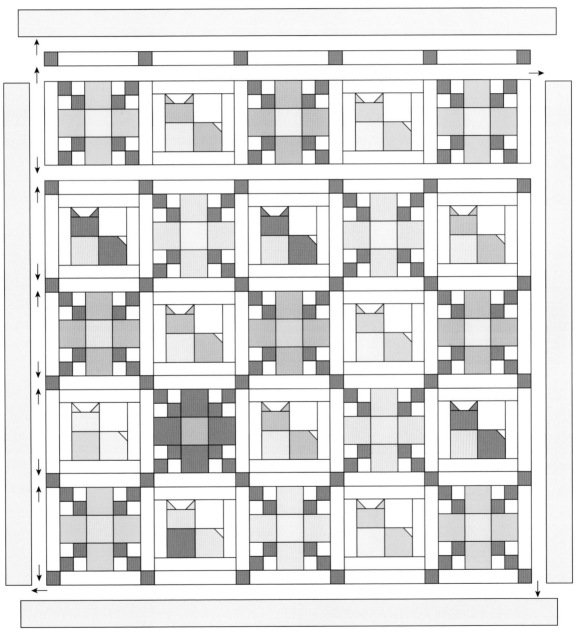

Quilt assembly

rise and shine

Growing up, I loved hearing stories from my Nana about life on the farm in Kansas. Some of Nana's farm chores included tending the sheep and feeding the chickens. Nana did not like the chickens; they would peck her little hands as she went to feed them. Living on a farm meant getting up early. When the rooster crowed, it was time to rise and shine!

materials

ASSORTED FAT QUARTERS: 16

WHITE SOLID: 1¼ yards for background

NAVY FLORAL: 1¼ yards for sashing and corners

ORANGE FLORAL: 1⅛ yards for borders (Add extra yardage for fussy cutting or matching prints.)

BINDING: ⅝ yard

BACKING: 4⅞ yards

BATTING: 73″ × 86″

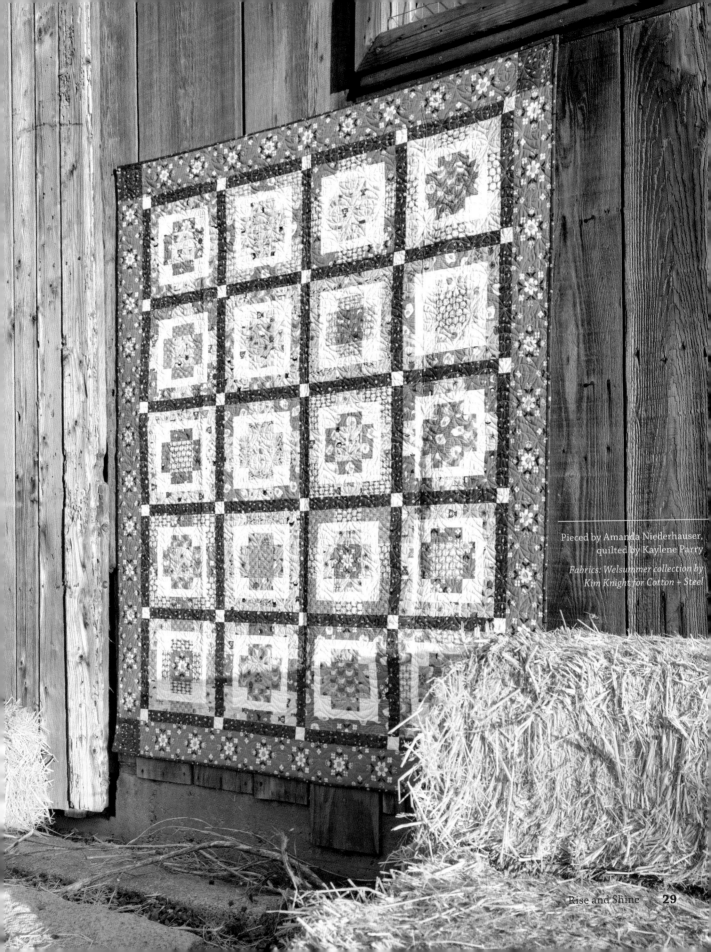

Pieced by Amanda Niederhauser,
quilted by Kaylene Parry

Fabrics: Welsummer collection by
Kim Knight for Cotton + Steel

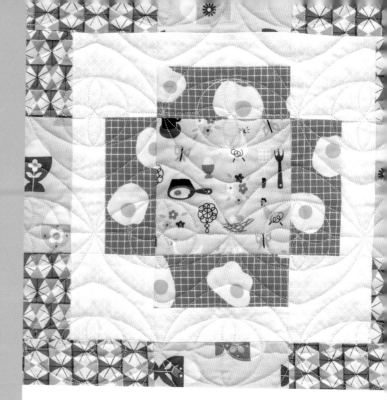

cutting

Assorted fat quarters

- From each of 12 fat quarters, cut 2 strips 4½″ × WOFQ (21″). Subcut into:

1 square 4½″ × 4½″ for the block center

12 rectangles 4½″ × 2″ for the center accents, border accents, and corners

4 rectangles 3″ × 2″ for the corners

Stack all same-size and same-print rectangles into sets of 4. Combine the smaller rectangle stack for the corners with 1 stack of 4 larger rectangles (4½″ × 2″) into a corner set.

- From each of 4 fat quarters, *carefully* cut *twice* (2 times) the number of pieces indicated for the fat quarters above.

White solid

- Cut 3 strips 4½″ × WOF and 1 strip 1½″ × WOF. Subcut into 80 rectangles 4½″ × 1½″.

- Cut 7 strips 3″ × WOF. Subcut into 80 squares 3″ × 3″.

- Cut 2 strips 2″ × WOF. Subcut into 30 squares 2″ × 2″ for the sashing cornerstones.

Navy floral

- Cut 2 strips 12½″ × WOF and 3 strips 2″ × WOF. Subcut into 49 sashing rectangles 12½″ × 2″.

- Cut 1 strip 5″ × WOF. Subcut into 4 squares 5″ × 5″ for the cornerstones.

Orange floral

- Cut 7 strips 5″ × WOF for the border.

Binding

- Cut 8 strips 2½″ × WOF.

Making the Rise and Shine Block

All seams are ¼″ unless otherwise noted. Follow the pressing arrows shown in the illustrations.

1. Choose fabrics for each of the 20 blocks and put them together in 20 piles. Select 4 different prints: 1 print for the center square, 2 large rectangle stacks in different prints, and 1 corner set in a fourth print. This makes block construction easy.

Each block pile will consist of:

- 1 print center square 4½″ × 4½″

- 2 different print stacks of large rectangles (1 stack each for center and border accents)

- 1 print corner set

- 4 white squares 3″ × 3″

- 4 white rectangles 4½″ × 1½″

2. Use the corner set and 4 white 3″ squares to make the corners. Sew the smaller 3″ × 2″ rectangles to the 3″ squares. Press. Make 4. **FIG. A**

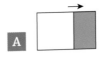

3. Sew the larger rectangles to the top of the corner units. One version will have the smaller rectangle on the left (A) and the other version will have it on the right (B). Press. Make 2 of each for a total of 4 corners. **FIG. B**

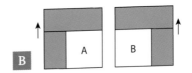

4. Use the 2 large rectangle stacks and the 4 white rectangles to make a side unit. Sew 2 large rectangles—1 from each stack—to either side of a white rectangle. Decide which print is the border accent and which is the center accent. Press the seams away from the border-accent print. Make a total of 4 side units. **FIG. C**

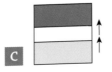

5. Lay out the block. Use 1 A corner and 1 B corner in rows 1 and 3. *Note the position of the large rectangle in each corner unit.* Orient the side units with the border accent print to the outside.

6. Sew the block together in rows. Press. Sew the rows together and press.

7. Repeat Steps 2–6 to make 20 blocks. **FIG. D**

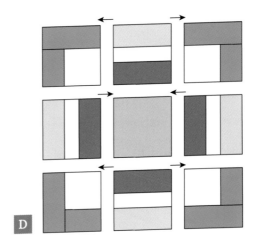

SASHING TIPS I like to use squares in my sashing because it helps keep the blocks nice and even. You don't always have to use a light color for the sashing. Try a dark color to make the blocks stand out.

Assembling the Quilt

1. To make a sashing row, sew 5 sashing cornerstones 2″ × 2″ between and at each end of 4 navy sashing rectangles 12½″ × 2″. Press. Make 6 sashing rows.

2. To make a block row, sew a navy sashing rectangle 12½″ × 2″ between and at each end of 4 blocks. Press. Make 5 block rows.

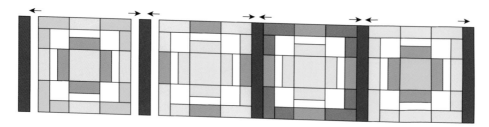

3. Lay out the quilt according to the quilt assembly diagram.

4. Sew the quilt together in rows, alternating the sashing rows and block rows.

5. Piece the 7 orange border strips together end to end. Subcut into 2 side borders 5″ × 69½″ and 2 top and bottom borders 5″ × 56″.

6. Sew the side borders to the quilt front.

7. Sew a 5″ navy square to both ends of the top and bottom borders. Press.

8. Sew the top and bottom borders to the quilt front.

Finishing

For more details, see Finishing (page 16).

1. Baste the quilt backing, batting, and quilt top together. Hand or machine quilt as desired. This quilt was machine quilted with a Vatican glass design.

2. Make the binding and attach it to the quilt.

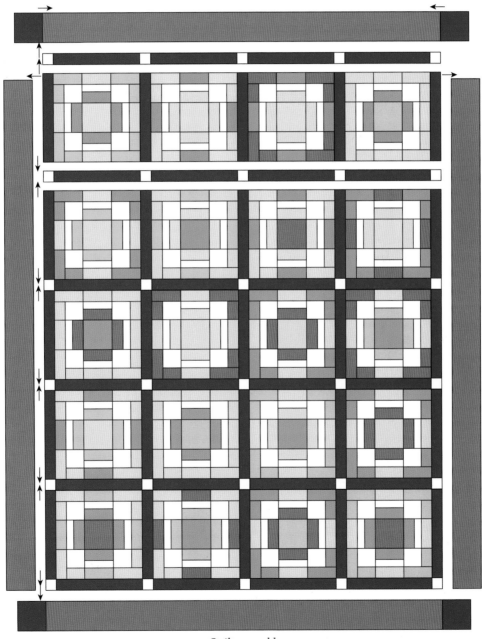

Quilt assembly

vintage treasures

I have loved vintage items before the word *vintage* was trendy. There is something satisfying about owning something that has a story. Maybe it's a way of holding onto the past, or maybe it's a way of wishing for simpler times. Whatever the reason, I can't get enough old stuff! My favorite collection is my vintage Pyrex dishes with their retro colors and fun shapes that delight me to no end. The colors in this quilt remind me of the colors commonly found in these dishes. The traditional Star and Pinwheel blocks in this quilt give it a nostalgic feel.

materials

10″ PRECUT SQUARES: 1 pack
including a minimum of the following:

    15 squares in assorted aqua prints

    15 squares in assorted gray prints

    4 squares in assorted pink prints

WHITE SOLID: 4 yards for background

PINK: 1¼ yards for border

BINDING: ⅝ yard (Or use extra the backing fabric for the binding.)

BACKING: 7⅜ yards

BATTING: 76″ × 88″

Pieced by Amanda Niederhauser,
quilted by Kaylene Parry

*Fabrics: Vintage Keepsakes collection by
Beverly McCullough for Riley Blake Designs*

cutting

10″ precut squares

- From each of 15 aqua squares, cut 8 squares 3″ × 3″ for the Pinwheel blocks.

- From each of 15 gray squares, cut:

  1 square 4½″ × 4½″ for the Star blocks

  8 squares 2½″ × 2½″ for the Star blocks

- From each of 4 pink squares, cut 4 center squares 4½″ × 4½″ for the Pinwheel blocks.

White solid

- Cut 10 strips 3″ × WOF. Subcut into 120 squares 3″ × 3″ for the Pinwheel blocks.

- Cut 23 strips 4½″ × WOF. Subcut into 180 squares 4½″ × 4½″ for the block backgrounds.

Pink

- Cut 8 strips 4½″ × WOF.

Binding

- Cut 8 strips 2½″ × WOF (or about 320″).

TIP I like to square up my half-square triangles so they are perfect. This pattern calls for making the half-square triangles from 3″ squares instead of the traditional 2⅞″ squares. Although it takes a bit more time, the results are worth it! Use a small cutting mat that rotates 360° for easier cutting.

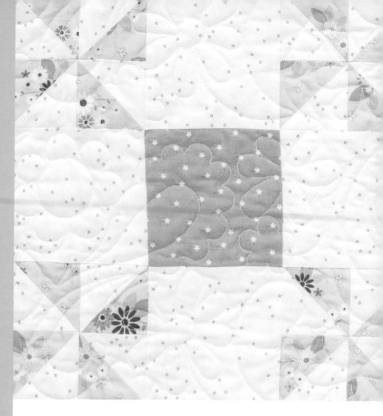

Making the Pinwheel Block

All seams are ¼″ unless otherwise noted. Follow the pressing arrows shown in the illustrations.

Note: The Pinwheel block consists of 4 pinwheels surrounding a center print square.

1. To make HSTs for the pinwheels, use 3″ aqua and white squares. Refer to Making Two Half-Square Triangles (page 15) for more information on the technique.

2. Square up the HSTs to measure 2½″ × 2½″. Repeat to make 240 HSTs.

3. Assemble the pinwheel unit by sewing 4 HSTs together as in a four-patch. Press the seams open. Make 60 pinwheel units. **FIG. A**

4. Lay out the Pinwheel block using 4 pinwheels, 4 background 4½″ squares, and 1 pink center square to form a nine-patch.

5. Sew the block together in rows. Press. Sew the rows together and press. Make 15 Pinwheel blocks.

FIG. B

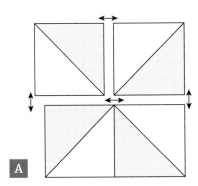

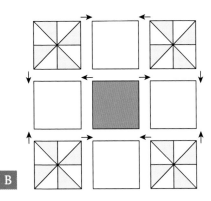

Making the Star Block

1. Draw a diagonal line on the wrong side of 120 gray 2½″ squares. Position one gray square on the corner of a 4½″ white square, RST.

2. Sew along the diagonal line. Cut ¼″ away from the diagonal line. Press.

3. Place another gray square from Step 1 on the adjacent corner, RST. Sew along the diagonal line. Trim ¼″ away from the seam. Press. Repeat to make 60 star-point units. FIG. C

4. Lay out the Star block by arranging 4 star-point units, 1 center gray 4½″ square, and 4 white 4½″ squares. Sew together as a nine-patch. Make 15 Star blocks. FIG. D

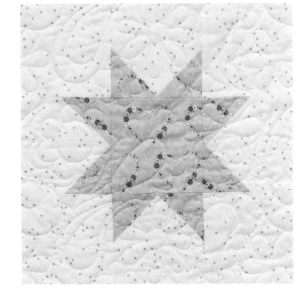

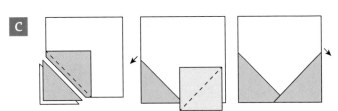

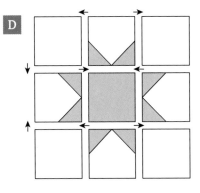

Assembling the Quilt

1. Lay out the Pinwheel and Star quilt blocks according to the diagram. Sew the blocks together in rows. Press toward the Star blocks. Sew the rows together and press in one direction.

2. Piece the pink border strips together end to end. Subcut into 2 side borders 4½″ × 72½″ and 2 top and bottom borders 4½″ × 68½″.

3. Sew the side borders to the quilt front. Press. Sew the top and bottom borders to the quilt front and press.

Finishing

For more details, see Finishing (page 16).

1. Baste the quilt backing, batting, and quilt top together. Hand or machine quilt as desired. This quilt was machine quilted with a floral design.

2. Make the binding and attach it to the quilt.

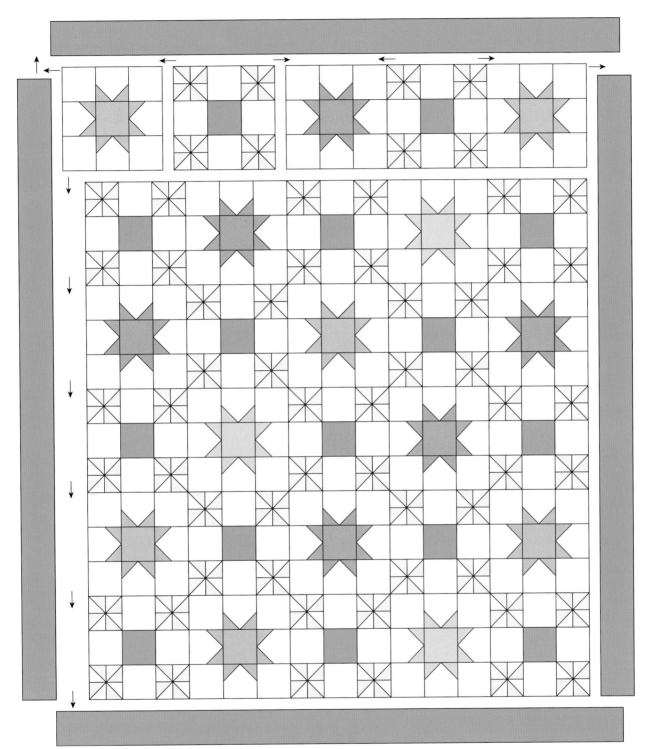

Quilt assembly

scrappy hearts

Heart quilts are my favorite! Maybe it's because I love love, or maybe it's because "love is all you need" and "love remains." Each heart that appears in this quilt is made up of four different fabrics, just like our own hearts are made up of many different aspects of our lives. Family, friends, Jesus, and pets are just a few parts of my personal scrappy heart. This is a wonderful quilt to give as a wedding or anniversary gift or to someone who needs to feel loved.

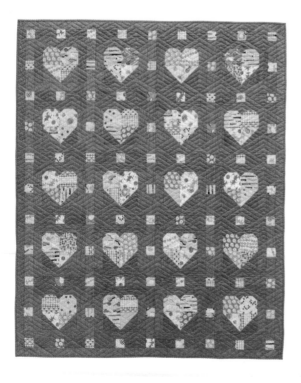

materials

5″ PRECUT SQUARES: 2 packs for hearts and cornerstones

DARK GRAY: 4¾ yards for background

BINDING: ⅝ yard

BACKING: 4 yards

BATTING: 70″ × 84″

TIP Don't be afraid to select a dark fabric as the background for a quilt. In this *Scrappy Hearts* quilt, the dark background fabric allows the lighter print fabrics to stand out.

Pieced by Amanda Niederhauser, quilted by Kaylene Parry

Fabrics: Trinket collection by Melody Miller for Cotton + Steel and Cross Weave by Moda Fabrics + Supplies

cutting

5″ precut squares

- Trim 40 squares to measure 4½″ × 4½″ for heart top units.

- Cut 20 squares into quarters to yield 80 squares 2½″ × 2½″ for the sashing cornerstones.

Dark gray

Scrappy Heart blocks

- Cut 3 strips 12½″ × WOF. Subcut into 40 rectangles 12½″ × 2½″.

- Cut 3 strips 8½″ × WOF. Subcut into 40 rectangles 8½″ × 2½″.

- Cut 3 strips 5″ × WOF. Subcut into 20 squares 5″ × 5″.

- Cut 3 strips 1½″ × WOF and use 1 scrap. Subcut into 80 squares 1½″ × 1½″. (Only 2 additional 1½″ squares are needed from the scrap.)

Sashing and borders

- Cut 6 strips 5½″ × WOF and 1 strip 2½″ × WOF. Subcut into 98 rectangles 5½″ × 2½″ for the block frames.

- Cut 8 strips 2½″ × WOF for the border.

Binding

- Cut 8 strips 2½″ × WOF.

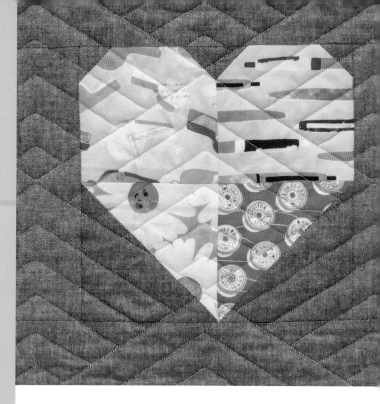

Making the Scrappy Heart Block

All seams are ¼″ unless otherwise noted. Follow the pressing arrows shown in the illustrations.

Combine heart top and bottom units and add a frame to make a Scrappy Heart block.

Making the Heart Top Units

1. Draw a diagonal line on the wrong side of 2 background 1½″ squares.

2. Position a background square on both top corners of a print 4½″ square. *Note the different angles of the diagonals.*

3. Sew on the diagonal line. Trim ½″ away from the seam and press open. Repeat to make 40 heart top units.

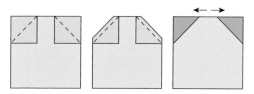

Making the Heart Bottom Units

1. To make HSTs for the bottom units, match a 5″ precut and background square. Refer to Making Two Half-Square Triangles (page 15) for more information on the technique.

2. Square up each HST to measure 4½″ × 4½″. Repeat to make 40 HSTs, or heart bottom units.

TIP Why a scant seam? Sewing half-square triangles can be tricky, and even the most experienced quilter can end up with uneven triangles. When sewing half-square triangles, it's best to make the largest HST possible so there is extra fabric for squaring up. By sewing a scant seam, the HST is slightly larger than necessary, which makes it easier to square up to the desired size.

Assembling the Block

1. Lay out the Scrappy Heart block using 2 heart top units and 2 heart bottom units.

2. Sew the block together as a four-patch, sewing the top 2 units together and the bottom 2 units together. Press the seams open. Sew the top unit to the bottom unit. Press the seams toward the top unit. FIG. A

3. Frame the scrappy heart by sewing an 8½″ background rectangle to both sides of the heart. Press. Sew a 12½″ background rectangle to the top and bottom of the heart and press. Repeat to make 20 Scrappy Heart blocks. FIG. B

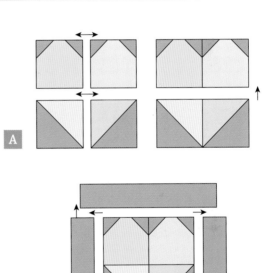

Making the Sashing

1. Sew a 2½″ print cornerstone square in between 2 background rectangles 5½″ × 2½″. Repeat to make 49 sashing units.

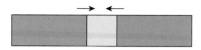

2. To make a sashing row, sew 5 print cornerstones between and at each end of 4 sashing units. Make 6 sashing rows.

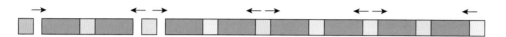

Assembling the Quilt

1. To make a block row, sew a sashing unit between and at each end of 4 blocks. Make 5 block rows.

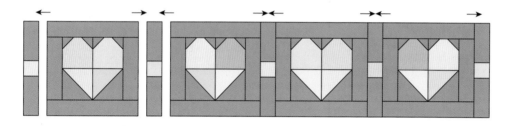

2. Sew the quilt together in rows, alternating the sashing and the block rows. Press the seams as indicated.

3. Piece the dark-gray border strips together end to end. Subcut into 2 side borders 2½″ × 72½″ and 2 top and bottom borders 2½″ × 62½″.

4. Sew the side borders to the quilt front. Sew the top and bottom borders to the quilt front. Press toward the borders.

Finishing

For more details, see Finishing (page 16).

1. Baste the quilt backing, batting, and quilt top together. Hand or machine quilt as desired. This quilt was machine quilted with a diamond fan design.

2. Make the binding and attach it to the quilt.

Quilt assembly

sunday drive

We recently had a super bloom in California. The hills were blanketed with fields of poppies and other wildflowers. On Sunday afternoons, we enjoyed driving up in the hills to see the colors up close. This quilt reminds me of those beautiful afternoons exploring nature.

materials

10″ PRECUT SQUARES: 1 pack in a variety of solids and prints

CREAM SOLID: 2⅝ yards for blocks, sashing, and inner border

NAVY FLORAL: 1 yard for outer border

BINDING: ⅝ yard

BACKING: 4⅓ yards

BATTING: 77″ × 77″

TIP I love that this quilt is made with 10″ squares and still features such a variety of color and patterns! Be sure to follow the 10″ square cutting instructions to get the most out of your precuts.

Pieced by Amanda Niederhauser,
quilted by Kaylene Parry

*Fabrics: Wild Bouquet collection by
Citrus & Mint Designs for Riley Blake Designs*

cutting

10″ precut squares

Where indicated, keep the cuts from each precut square together as a set.

- Choose 16 squares. Subcut *each* into 8 squares 2½″ × 2½″ and 4 rectangles 4½″ × 2½″ as a block's frame set.

2½″	2½″	2½″ × 4½″

- Choose 9 squares. Subcut *each* into 1 square 3½″ × 3½″ and 8 squares 2″ × 2″ as a sashing star set.
- Choose 8 squares. Subcut *each* into 16 squares 2½″ × 2½″ as 2 Flying Geese sets of 8 squares each.
- Choose 4 squares. Subcut *each* into 4 squares 4½″ × 4½″ for the block centers.

Cream solid

- Cut 2 strips 12½″ × WOF and 1 strip 3½″ × WOF. Subcut into 24 sashing rectangles 12½″ × 3½″.
- Cut 4 strips 4½″ × WOF. Subcut into 64 rectangles 4½″ × 2½″ for the Flying Geese.
- Cut 15 strips 2½″ × WOF.

Set 7 strips aside for the inner border.

Subcut 8 strips into 128 squares 2½″ × 2½″ for the four-patches.

Navy floral

- Cut 8 strips 4½″ × WOF for the outer border.

Binding

- Cut 8 strips 2½″ × WOF.

Making the Flower Block

All seams are ¼″ unless otherwise noted. Follow the pressing arrows shown in the illustrations.

Each block features 3 different prints for the center, frame, and Flying Geese points.

Choose fabrics for each of the 16 blocks and put them together into 16 piles. This makes block construction easy.

Each block pile will consist of:

- 1 block center
- 1 block frame set
- 1 Flying Geese set
- 8 cream squares 2½″ × 2½″
- 4 cream rectangles 4½″ × 2½″

Making the Four-Patch Units

1. Pair 8 cream squares with 8 squares from the block frame set. Sew each pair RST. Press.

2. Use 2 pairs to make a four-patch unit. Make 4 four-patch units. Following the diagram, orient the four-patches as shown and press accordingly for 2 four-patches of each orientation. FIG. A

Making the Flying Geese Units

1. Draw a diagonal line on the wrong side of the 8 squares from the Flying Geese set.

2. Position a square on a cream rectangle, RST at one end. Sew along the diagonal line.

3. Trim ¼″ away from the diagonal line. Press. FIG. B

4. Repeat Steps 2 and 3 on the opposite end of the rectangle. Make 4 Flying Geese units. FIG. C

5. Sew 1 rectangle from the block's frame set to the bottom of each Flying Geese unit. Press. Repeat to make 4 side units. FIG. D

Assembling the Block

Lay out the block as a nine-patch. Be mindful of the orientation of the units. Sew the units together in rows and then the rows together to complete a block. Make 16 blocks. FIG. E

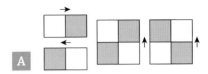

A

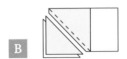

B

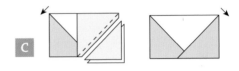

C

D

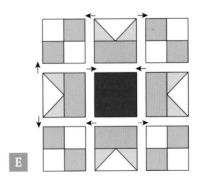

E

Making the Sashing

1. Lay out the 16 quilt blocks in 4 rows of 4 blocks each. Place a sashing rectangle 12½″ × 3½″ in between each block. From the 9 sashing star sets, place the 3½″ star squares as sashing cornerstones. FIG. F

TIP At this point, the quilt layout looks traditional with its blocks and sashing. By adding star points to the sashing rectangles, the quilt becomes more interesting, and a secondary pattern is created with stars. The points on the sashing rectangles are constructed just like the Flying Geese. Make sure the points and the cornerstones are from the same fabric.

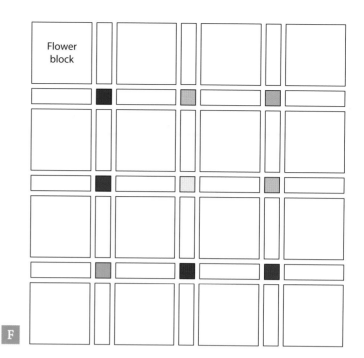

F

2. On each side of a star cornerstone square, star points are added to the sashing rectangles. Use the matching set of 8 star point 2″ squares to add points to the adjacent 4 sashing rectangles: Draw a diagonal line on the wrong side of 2 star point 2″ squares. Align a square RST to the bottom corner of a sashing rectangle 12½″ × 3½″. Sew on the diagonal line. Trim off the corner, leaving a ¼″ seam allowance. Repeat on the adjacent corner with the second star point square.

3. Repeat the technique described in Step 2 to add all the star points to the sashing rectangles. Some sashing rectangles will have star points *at both ends*.

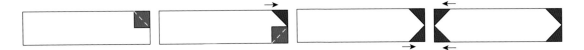

4. Sew 3 horizontal sashing rows together by alternating sashing units and star squares. Press seams open.

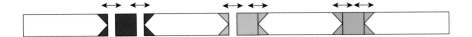

Assembling the Quilt

1. Sew the Flower block rows together. There are 4 rows of 4 blocks alternating with 3 vertical sashing units.

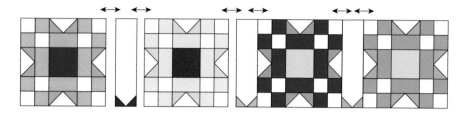

2. Sew 4 block rows together with 3 sashing rows between them, as shown. Press open.

3. Piece 7 inner border strips together end to end. Subcut into 2 side inner borders 2½″ × 57½″ and 2 top and bottom inner borders 2½″ × 61½″.

4. Sew the side inner borders to the quilt front. Press. Sew the top and bottom inner borders to the quilt front and press.

5. Piece the 8 outer border strips together end to end. Subcut into 2 side outer borders 4½″ × 61½″ and 2 top and bottom outer borders 4½″ × 69½″.

6. Sew the side outer borders to the quilt front. Press. Sew the outer top and bottom borders to the quilt front and press.

Finishing

For more details, see Finishing (page 16).

1. Baste the quilt backing, batting, and quilt top together. Hand or machine quilt as desired. This quilt was machine quilted with a floral design.

2. Make the binding and attach it to the quilt.

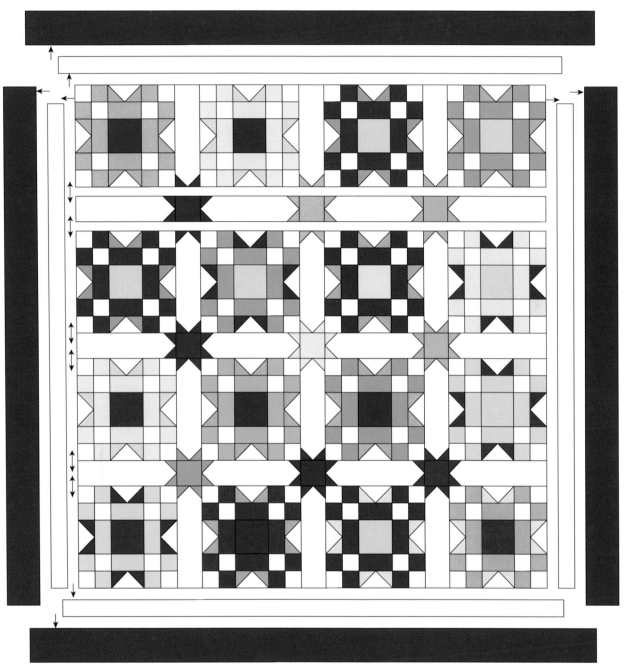

Quilt assembly

gingham patches

As a child during the 70s, I grew up with gingham all around me! My dresses, my bedding, my wallpaper, my doll clothes, and my lunch box were all gingham. I suppose my current love for gingham is rooted in my happy childhood memories. As an adult, my gingham obsession has far surpassed my childhood love. I have gingham shoes, purses, blouses, dresses, jackets, bedding, dishes, and pillows—need I go on? This quilt is a little tribute to my total and complete love for all things gingham.

materials

ASSORTED GINGHAM FAT EIGHTHS: 8 for block centers (I used light pink, dark gray, orange, light blue, aqua, dark pink, light green, and dark teal.)

ASSORTED SOLID 2½″-WIDE PRECUT STRIPS (OR 10″ SQUARES): 20 to match gingham colors for block corners. Select 2 strips for 4 colors and 3 strips for the remaining 4 colors. Each strip will make 1 block.

GRAY SOLID: 1 roll of 2½″-wide precut strips *or* 2 yards for block background

WHITE SOLID: 1 roll of 2½″-wide precut strips *or* 2 yards for blocks and sashing

BINDING: ⅝ yard

BACKING: 3⅔ yards

BATTING: 66″ × 80″

TIP This quilt uses ginghams for the block centers. How about trying all polka dots or stripes? It's easy to switch out the block centers to use your favorite fabric patterns. Also watch for 5″ square packs that are specially curated by local quilt shops or online quilt shops. These may have more variety and have fabrics from many different designers.

Pieced by Amanda Niederhauser, quilted by Kaylene Parry

Fabrics: Ginghams and solids from Cotton + Steel

cutting

Assorted gingham fat eighths

• Cut 2 or 3 squares 4½″ × 4½″ from each gingham color based on the number of solid matching strips (or 10″ squares) for a total of 20 center squares.

Assorted solid 2½″-wide precut strips (or 10″ squares)

• Cut 14 squares 2½″ × 2½″ from each.

Pair every 12 squares with a matching 4½″ gingham center square for each block. Extra solid squares are used as cornerstones for the sashing.

Gray solid

• If using yardage, cut 25 strips 2½″ × WOF.

From 15 strips, subcut 240 squares 2½″ × 2½″.

From 10 strips, subcut 80 rectangles 4½″ × 2½″.

White solid

• If using yardage, cut 27 strips 2½″ × WOF.

From 17 strips, subcut 49 sashing rectangles 12½″ × 2½″.

From 10 strips subcut 80 rectangles 4½″ × 2½″.

Binding

• Cut 7 strips 2½″ × WOF.

Making the Gingham Block

All seams are ¼″ unless otherwise noted. Follow the pressing arrows shown in the illustrations.

1. Sew 80 gray and 80 white 4½″ × 2½″ rectangles RST lengthwise to make all the side units used in the blocks. Press. **FIG. A**

2. For each block, you will need:

• 1 gingham center square

• 12 matching 2½″ solid squares

• 12 gray 2½″ squares

• 4 side units

3. To make the 8 half-square triangles needed for the corners, use 8 gray and 8 matching solid 2½″ squares. Refer to Making One Half-Square Triangle (page 15) for more information on the technique. Press. Repeat to make 8 HST units.

4. Make a corner four-patch unit with 1 gray and 1 matching solid 2½˝ square, and 2 HSTs. Press all seams open. Make 4 corner units. FIG. B

5. Lay out the block elements: 1 gingham center square, 4 side units, and 4 corner units. Sew the units together into rows and then the rows together to make 1 block. Press. FIG. C

6. Repeat Steps 2–5 to make 20 blocks.

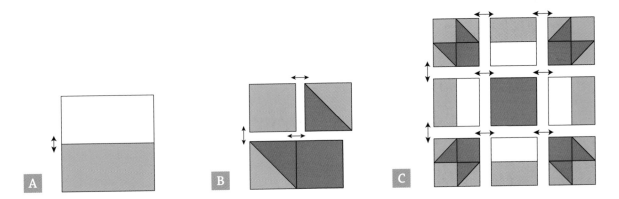

Assembling the Quilt

1. To make a sashing row, sew 5 assorted 2½˝ cornerstones between and at each end of 4 sashing rectangles 12½˝ × 2½˝. Make 6 sashing rows.

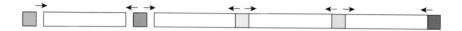

2. To make a block row, sew 5 sashing rectangles 12½˝ × 2½˝ between and at each end of 4 blocks. Press. Make 5 block rows.

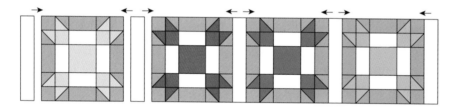

3. Sew the quilt together in rows, alternating the sashing rows and block rows.

Finishing

For more details, see Finishing (page 16).

1. Baste the quilt backing, batting, and quilt top together. Hand or machine quilt as desired. This quilt was machine quilted with a pineapple skin design.

2. Make the binding and attach it to the quilt.

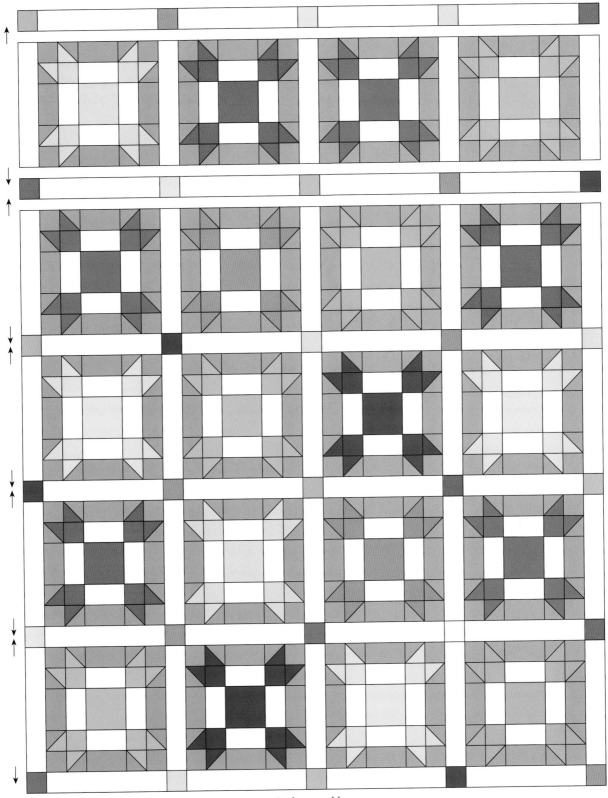

Quilt assembly

colonial flowers

I fell in love with quilting when I lived in Arlington, Virginia. One day I went over to my friend Anna's house and she showed me a baby quilt she was making. I could not believe my eyes! The cutest fabric I'd ever seen had been cut into pieces and then resewn into a darling quilt. I wanted in! The very next week I found a quilt shop, bought some books, and bought lots of fabric. I was hooked for life.

I was also blessed to meet my friend Linda while living in Virginia as well. Linda was my mentor for the early years of my adulthood. She was an artist, quilt designer, decorator, antique expert, cat lover, and she was fabulous at everything she did. She encouraged my beginning quilting attempts and helped me along the way. I still feel her influence in my life today! This quilt reminds me of Virginia: the patriotic colors, the antique feel of the fabrics, and the traditional quilt block.

materials

ASSORTED RED 2½″-WIDE PRECUT STRIPS: 1 roll for blocks

AQUA FLORAL: 1⅛ yards for block centers and border

WHITE DOT: 2½ yards for background

NAVY FLORAL: ⅞ yard for sashing

BINDING: ⅝ yard

BACKING: 3⅞ yards

BATTING: 69″ × 69″

Pieced by Amanda Niederhauser,
quilted by Kaylene Parry

*Fabrics: Hedge Rose collection by
Kelly Panacci and So Ruby collection by
Carina Gardner, both for
Riley Blake Designs*

cutting

Assorted red 2½″-wide precut strips

- From 14 strips, cut 108 rectangles 4½″ × 2½″.

- From 3 strips, cut 36 squares 2½″ × 2½″.

Aqua floral

- Cut 2 strips 4½″ × WOF. Subcut into 9 squares 4½″ × 4½″ for the block centers.

- Cut 6 strips 4″ × WOF for the borders.

White dot

- Cut 16 strips 2½″ × WOF. Subcut into 252 squares 2½″ × 2½″ for the blocks.

- Cut 20 strips 2″ × WOF for the sashing strip sets and nine-patches.

Navy floral

- Cut 13 strips 2″ × WOF for the sashing strip sets and nine-patches.

Binding

- Cut 7 strips 2½″ × WOF.

TIP Pressing seams open can seem like a pain. It takes longer, and you might even burn your fingers along the way! But don't skip this important step. This particular quilt comes together with more ease and lies flat because of the open seams. I like to press the seams to one side first and then press the seams open.

Making the Colonial Flower Block

All seams are ¼″ unless otherwise noted. Follow the pressing arrows shown in the illustrations.

Making the Corner Units

1. To make HSTs for the blocks' corner units, place 1 red and 1 white 2½″ square RST. Refer to Making One Half-Square Triangle (page 15) for more information on the technique. Make 36 HSTs.

2. Add a 2½″ white square to the HSTs to make 2 versions of half-square rectangle units. Note the position of the HSTs. Make 18 with the red half of the HST on the right and 18 with the red half of the HST on the left, as shown. Make a total of 36 half-square rectangle units. **FIG. A**

3. Select 36 red rectangles 4½″ × 2½″ and 36 white 2½″ squares. Draw a diagonal line on the wrong side of the white squares.

4. RST, place a white square at one end of a red rectangle. Have the diagonal line going from the top left to the bottom right. Sew on the drawn line and trim ¼˝ away from the seam. Press open. Make 18 rectangle units. FIG. B

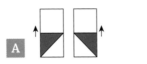

5. Repeat Step 3 with the remaining 18 red rectangles and white squares, but this time have the diagonal going from the top right to the bottom left. Make 18 rectangle units reversed. FIG. C

6. To make a corner unit, sew a rectangle unit with a diagonal going from the top left to the bottom right RST with a half-square rectangle unit with the same diagonal. Make 18 corner A units. FIG. D

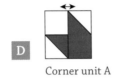 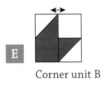

Corner unit A   Corner unit B

7. Repeat Step 6 but with the diagonals going in the opposite direction, and sew the rectangle unit to the left side. Make 18 corner B units. FIG. E

Making the Center Units

1. Use the same method as in Making the Corner Units, Steps 3–5 (previous page and above), but this time, sew a white square to *both* ends of a red rectangle. Make 36 with both diagonals going from the top left to the bottom right and 36 with both diagonals going from the top right to the bottom left. FIG. F

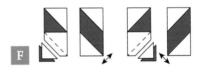

2. To complete a center unit, sew 2 rectangles with opposing diagonals together lengthwise. Press open. Make 36 center units. FIG. G

Assembling the Block

Assemble the block as a nine-patch, arranging 2 corner A units, 2 corner B units, 4 center units, and 1 center square. Sew the units together in rows and then sew the rows together. Press all seams open. Make 9 blocks. FIG. H

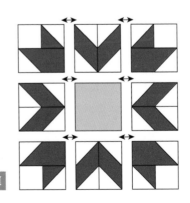

Playful Precut Quilts

Making the Sashing

Making the Strip Sets

1. To make a strip set, sew a white dot strip 2″ × WOF to both sides of a navy strip 2″ × WOF. Press the seams toward the navy strip. Make 9 strip sets. From 1 strip set, subcut 16 segments each 2″ wide. Set aside for the sashing nine-patches. From the remaining 8 strip sets, subcut 24 sashing strips each 12½″ long.

2. Sew a navy strip 2″ × WOF to both sides of a white dot strip 2″ × WOF. Press toward the navy strips. Make 2 strip sets. Subcut 32 segments each 2″ wide for the sashing nine-patches.

Making the Sashing Nine-Patches and Rows

1. Sew a 2″ white/navy/white strip segment between 2 navy/white/navy 2″ strip segments to form a nine-patch unit, as shown. Press open. Make 16.

2. To make a sashing row, sew 4 nine-patch units between and at each end of 3 sashing 12½″ units. Make 4 sashing rows.

Assembling the Quilt

1. To make a block row, sew 4 sashing units between and at the end of 3 blocks. Make 3 rows.

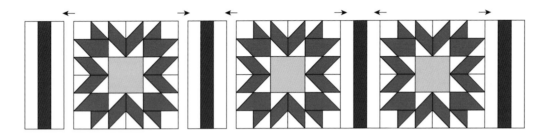

2. Sew the sashing rows and block rows together, matching seams at each intersection. Press toward the sashing.

3. Piece 6 aqua floral border strips together end to end. Subcut into 2 side borders 4″ × 54½″ and 2 top and bottom borders 4″ × 61½″.

4. Sew the side borders to the quilt front. Press. Sew the top and bottom borders to the quilt front and press.

Finishing

For more details, see Finishing (page 16).

1. Baste the quilt backing, batting, and quilt top together. Hand or machine quilt as desired. This quilt was machine quilted with a floral design.

2. Make the binding and attach it to the quilt.

Quilt assembly

newport beach

I am a California girl. I grew up going to Newport Beach during the summers with family and friends. As a mom, Newport Beach is a place I love taking my children. The pier, The Wedge, Balboa Bars—nothing has changed over the years. I love driving over the bridge through the harbor. There are flags flying, boats sailing, and often sea lions playing! This quilt feels like the harbor with nautical colors and crisp white backgrounds. It's a perfect size to take on the boat or to the beach!

materials

FAT EIGHTHS: 20 for blocks. Select 5 assorted prints from *each* of the following 4 colors: navy blue, red, medium blue, and mint/aqua.

MEDIUM BLUE: 1½ yards for sashing, border, and binding

WHITE SOLID: 2⅞ yards for border, blocks, and sashing

BACKING: 4⅞ yards

BATTING: 72″ × 86″

TIP I love working with fat eighths because I can cut a fat quarter in half and still have a good-size piece left over. If you don't have precut fat eighths, you can cut them yourself.

Pieced by Amanda Niederhauser,
quilted by Kaylene Parry

*Fabrics: By the Sea collection
by Dani Mogstad for Riley Blake Designs*

cutting

Fat eighths

- Cut *each* of the 20 fat eighths into:

2 squares 4″ × 4″ to make 1 HST set

4 rectangles 6½″ × 3½″ to make 1 block frame set

1 square 2½″ × 2½″ for the block center

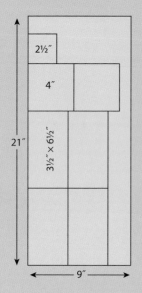

Medium blue

- Cut 8 strips 3½″ × WOF. Subcut into 120 rectangles 3½″ × 2½″ for the sashing and border.

- Cut 8 strips 2½″ × WOF for the binding.

White solid

- Cut 1 strip 12½″ × WOF and 3 strips 3½″ × WOF. Subcut into 18 rectangles 12½″ × 3½″ for the border and 4 squares 3½″ × 3½″ for the border cornerstones.

- Cut 6 strips 6½″ × WOF. Subcut into 89 rectangles 6½″ × 2½″ for the block centers and sashing.

- Cut 4 strips 4″ × WOF. Subcut into 40 squares 4″ × 4″ for the block HSTs.

- Cut 5 strips 2½″ × WOF. Subcut into 70 squares 2½″ × 2½″ for the block centers and sashing cornerstones.

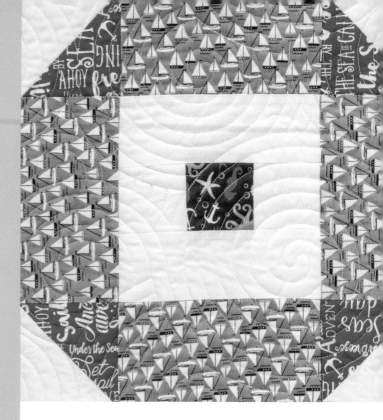

Making the Newport Beach Block

All seams are ¼″ unless otherwise noted. Follow the pressing arrows shown in the illustrations.

1. To make a block center, sew a 2½″ white square to both sides of a 2½″ print square. Press. Sew a white rectangle 6½″ × 2½″ to the top and bottom of the square unit. Press. Make 20 block centers.

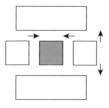

2. To make the 4 corner HSTs, pair 2 white 4″ squares with 1 HST set of print squares. Refer to Making Two Half-Square Triangles (page 15) for more information on the technique.

3. Square up the 4 HSTs to measure 3½″ × 3½″. Keep the 4 HSTs together as 1 set. Make 20 sets of HSTs.

Assembling the Block

1. For each block, select 3 different prints for the block elements: center, HSTs, and frame.

2. Lay out the block center, 4 HSTs, and a block frame set of 4 rectangles 6½″ × 3½″, as shown.

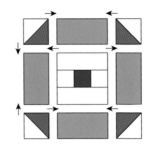

3. Sew the block together in rows. Press as shown.

4. Sew the rows together. Press.

5. Repeat Steps 1–4 to make 20 blocks.

Assembling the Quilt

Making the Sashing

1. Sew a medium-blue sashing rectangle 3½″ × 2½″ to each side of a white sashing rectangle 6½″ × 2½″. Press. Repeat to make 49 sashing units.

2. To make a sashing row, sew 5 white 2½″ sashing cornerstones between and at the end of 4 sashing units. Press as indicated. Make 6 sashing rows.

Making the Block Rows

1. To make a block row, sew 5 sashing units between and at the end of 4 blocks. Press as indicated. Make 5 block rows.

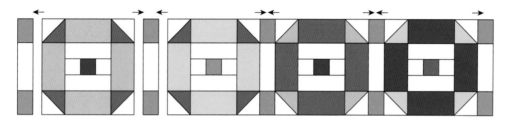

2. Sew the quilt together in rows, alternating the sashing rows and blocks rows, and matching seams at each intersection. Press to the sashing.

Making the Border

1. To make a side border, sew 6 medium-blue border rectangles 3½″ × 2½″ between and at the end of 5 white border rectangles 12½″ × 3½″. Press as shown. Make 2.

2. Sew the side borders to the quilt front. Press.

3. To make each top and bottom border, sew 5 blue border rectangles 3½″ × 2½″ between and at the end of 4 white border rectangles 12½″ × 3½″. Sew a 3½″ white cornerstone to each end. Press as shown.

4. Sew the top and bottom borders to the quilt front. Press.

Finishing

For more details, see Finishing (page 16).

1. Baste the quilt backing, batting, and quilt top together. Hand or machine quilt as desired. This quilt was machine quilted with a circle design.

2. Make the binding and attach it to the quilt.

Quilt assembly

flower basket

This quilt is designed with partial seams to give it a woven look—just like a basket! You cannot tell where the block pieces begin and end. If you are new to partial seams, don't worry. Sewing a partial seam just means you sew a seam partway and finish sewing it later.

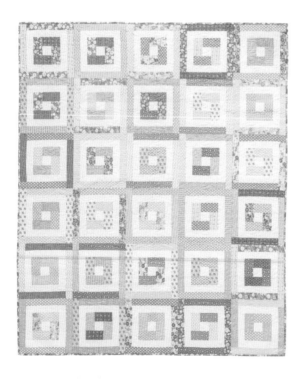

materials

2½″-WIDE PRECUT STRIPS: 2 high-volume print rolls *or* 60 strips 2½″ × WOF

WHITE SOLID: 1¾ yards

BINDING: ⅝ yard

BACKING: 3⅞ yards

BATTING: 68″ × 80″

Pieced by Amanda Niederhauser,
quilted by Kaylene Parry

Fabrics: Lollipop Garden collection
by Lella Boutique for Moda Fabrics + Supplies

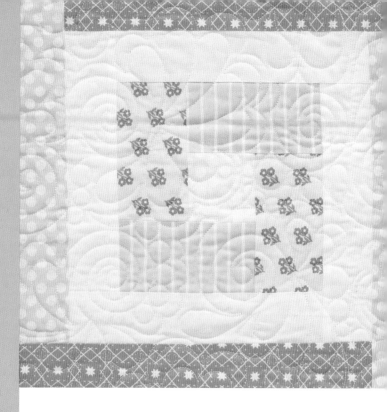

cutting

2½"-wide precut strips

Keep all print rectangles organized in pairs by size.

- From each of 30 high-volume strips, cut:

  2 rectangles 11" × 2"

  4 rectangles 4½" × 2½"

- From each of 30 high-volume strips, cut 2 rectangles 11" × 2".

White solid

- Cut 2 strips 2½" × WOF. Subcut into 30 squares 2½" × 2½" for the block centers.

- Cut 6 strips 8" × WOF. Subcut into 120 rectangles 8" × 2".

Binding

- Cut 8 strips 2½" × WOF.

TIP Partial seams allow this frame-style block to have only one rectangle measurement for each frame. Make sure to press only the partial seam at first, and then press the whole seam once it's complete.

Making the Flower Basket Block

All seams are ¼" unless otherwise noted. Follow the pressing arrows shown in the illustrations.

1. Select a 2½" white center square and 2 different pairs of print rectangles 4½" × 2½" in the same colorway.

2. Sew a rectangle to the right side of the center square, lining up the top edges. The rectangle will be longer than the side of the square. Sew from the top to halfway down the square, making a partial seam. Press only the partial seam toward the rectangle. **FIG. A**

3. Using the second print, sew the next rectangle across the seam just sewn. It will fit across the top edge. Continue sewing rectangles to the edge of the square, alternating prints and pressing after each seam. **FIG. B**

4. Returning to the first rectangle, sew the remainder of the partial seam to complete the round. Press. FIG. C

5. In the same manner as in Steps 2–4, sew 4 white rectangles 8″ × 2″ to each side of the block, beginning with a partial seam and ending by completing the partial seam. Press toward the white fabric.

6. In the same manner as in Steps 2–4, sew 2 different pairs of print rectangles 11″ × 2″ to each side of the block, beginning with a partial seam and ending by completing the partial seam. Press toward the rectangles. Make 30 blocks. FIG. D

Assembling the Quilt

1. Lay out the quilt in 6 rows of 5 blocks each.

2. Sew the blocks together in rows. Press the rows in alternate directions.

3. Sew the rows together, matching seams at each intersection. Press in one direction.

Finishing

For more details, see Finishing (page 16).

1. Baste the quilt backing, batting, and quilt top together. Hand or machine quilt as desired. This quilt was machine quilted with a floral design.

2. Make the binding and attach it to the quilt.

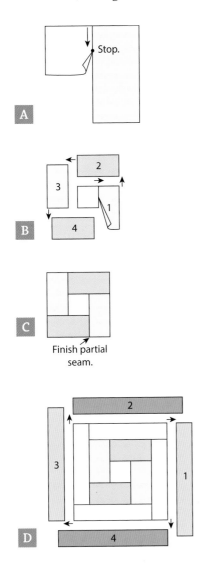

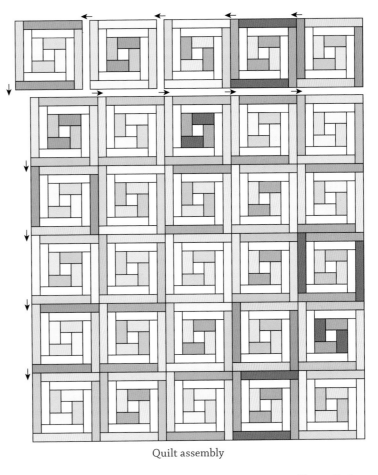

Quilt assembly

summer picnic

Summer is my favorite season. Maybe it's because I have a July birthday; maybe it's because I love the beach; or maybe it's because it's the time when my family gathers for picnics, fireworks, BBQs, homemade ice cream, peach picking, and swim parties. It's the *best*! In northern California, the summer evenings are usually cool and require sweatshirts and quilts. The colors and design of this quilt are reminiscent of summer evenings watching fireworks while eating fresh peach pie and ice cream.

materials

2½″-WIDE PRECUT STRIPS: 1 roll including the following:

  14 navy strips (7 matching print pairs)

  6 red strips

  6 tan strips

  6 light blue strips

CREAM SOLID: 2⅞ yards for background

MEDIUM BLUE: 1⅛ yards for outer border

BINDING: ⅝ yard

BACKING: 4⅞ yards

BATTING: 73″ × 87″

Pieced by Amanda Niederhauser, quilted by Kaylene Parry

Fabrics: Sweet Tea collection by Sweetwater for Moda Fabrics + Supplies

cutting

2½″-wide precut strips

Keep all cuts organized by print in 20 sets of 4, except for the light blue squares. The extra fabric allotted for the red, tan, and light blue squares allows for more variety in the print selection.

- From 14 navy strips, cut 80 rectangles 6½″ × 2½″.
- From 6 red strips, cut 80 squares 2½″ × 2½″.
- From 6 tan strips, cut 80 squares 2½″ × 2½″.
- From 6 light blue strips, cut 60 squares 2½″ × 2½″.

Cream solid

- Cut 1 strip 10½″ × WOF. Subcut into 14 rectangles 10½″ × 2½″ for the sashing.
- Cut 1 strip 8½″ × WOF and use 1 scrap. Subcut into 17 rectangles 8½″ × 2½″ for the sashing.
- Cut 5 strips 6½″ × WOF. Subcut into 80 rectangles 6½″ × 2½″ for the blocks and sashing.
- Cut 10 strips 2½″ × WOF. Subcut into 160 squares 2½″ × 2½″ for the blocks.
- Cut 6 strips 2″ × WOF for the inner border.

Medium blue

- Cut 8 strips 4½″ × WOF for the outer border.

Binding

- Cut 8 strips 2½″ × WOF.

Making the Summer Picnic Block

All seams are ¼″ unless otherwise noted. Follow pressing arrows shown in the illustrations.

1. Select 8 cream squares, 4 cream 6½″ rectangles, a set of navy rectangles, a set of red squares, and a set of tan squares.

2. Draw a diagonal line on the wrong side of a cream square. Place the square RST on a navy rectangle, aligning at one end. Pay close attention to the angle of the diagonal.

3. Sew on the diagonal line. Trim off the corners, leaving a ¼″ seam allowance. Press the seam open. Make 4 identical triangle units. **FIG. A**

4. Sew a red, tan, and cream 2½″ square together in that order, as shown. Press the seams in one direction. Make 4 identical triple-square units. **FIG. B**

5. Sew a 6½" cream rectangle, a triple-square unit, and a triangle unit together. Press. Make 4 identical quarter-block units. FIG. C

6. Lay out 4 identical quarter-block units into a four-patch, forming an on-point cream square in the center. Sew the top 2 units together. Press. Sew the bottom 2 units together. Press. Sew the top and bottom units together, matching the center seam intersection. Press the seams open. Make 20 blocks. FIG. D

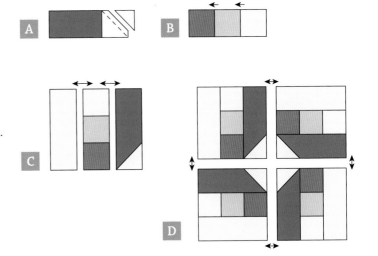

Making the Sashing

1. Sew a 2½" light blue square to a 10½" sashing rectangle. Press. Make 14 sashing A units.

Sashing A

2. Sew 2 light blue 2½" squares to each end of an 8½" sashing rectangle. Press. Make 17 sashing B units.

Sashing B

3. To make a sashing row, sew 3 light blue 2½" squares between and at the end of 2 sashing B units. Add a sashing A unit to each end to complete the sashing row. Press. Make 4 sashing rows.

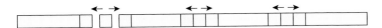

TIP Quilt sashing can add a design element just like quilt blocks. In this quilt, the sashing units and sashing corners come together to form a pattern, which adds interest to the quilt. Play around with different colors and intensities to get different looks.

Assembling the Quilt

1. To make block rows 2, 3, and 4, sew 3 sashing B units between 4 blocks. Press.

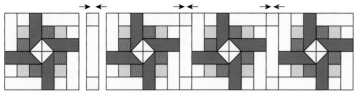

Block rows 2, 3, and 4

2. To make block rows 1 and 5, sew 3 sashing A units between 4 blocks. (In the quilt, block row 5 will be turned 180°.)

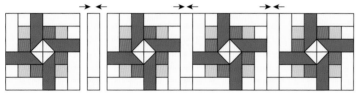

Block rows 1 and 5

3. Sew 4 sashing rows between 5 block rows. Press toward the sashing rows.

4. Sew the 6 cream inner border strips end to end. Subcut into 2 side inner borders 2″ × 68½″ and 2 top and bottom inner borders 2″ × 57½″.

5. Sew the side inner borders to the quilt front. Press toward the inner borders. Sew the top and bottom inner borders to the quilt front. Press toward the inner borders.

6. Sew the 8 medium-blue border strips end to end. Subcut into 2 side outer borders 4½″ × 71½″ and 2 top and bottom outer borders 4½″ × 65½″.

7. Sew the side outer borders to the quilt front. Press toward the outer borders. Sew the top and bottom outer borders to the quilt front. Press toward the outer borders.

Finishing

For more details, see Finishing (page 16).

1. Baste the quilt backing, batting, and quilt top together. Hand or machine quilt as desired. This quilt was machine quilted with diagonal plaid design.

2. Make the binding and attach it to the quilt.

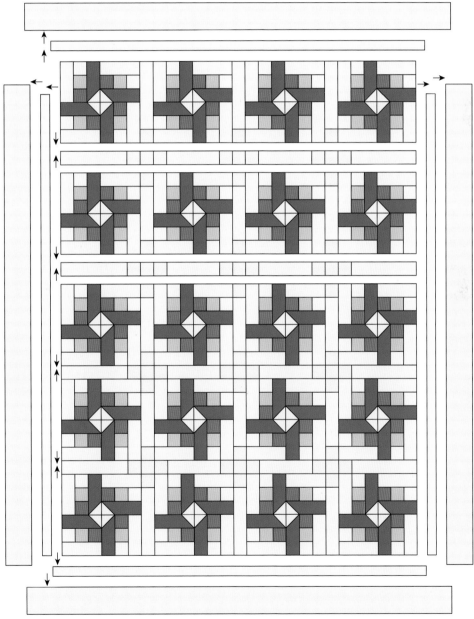

Quilt assembly

leaf peeping

When we lived in Virginia, our favorite time of the year was fall. The humidity died down, the skies were blue, and the leaves were spectacular! A common fall pastime in Virginia is to go "leaf peeping." We loved packing up the car and driving to an area rich in foliage to spend the day. At home we would pile up leaves and the children would run and jump in them. This quilt reminds me of those memorable fall days.

materials

5″ PRECUT SQUARES: 4 packs *or* 1 pack of 10″ precut squares that contain the following colors: yellow, brown, green, aqua, gray, orange, and red

WHITE SOLID: 3⅞ yards

BINDING: ⅔ yard

BACKING: 5⅛ yards

BATTING: 80″ × 92″

Pieced by Amanda Niederhauser, quilted by Kaylene Parry

Fabrics: Autumn Love collection by Lori Holt for Riley Blake Designs and Basics collection from Riley Blake Designs

cutting

If you choose the pack of 10″ precut squares, cut each square into quarters, yielding 168 squares 5″ × 5″.

Separate the 5″ squares into the following color piles:

Yellow, brown, green, aqua, and gray: 16 squares each

Orange: 22 squares

Red: 20 squares

5″ precut squares

From each of the yellow, brown, green, aqua, and gray color piles:

- Set aside 4 squares for the leaf HSTs.

- Cut 10 squares into quarters, yielding 40 squares 2½″ × 2½″ for the four-patches in both blocks.

- Trim 2 squares to 4½″ × 4½″ for the leaf stems.

From the orange pile:

- Set aside 6 squares for the leaf HSTs.

- Cut 13 squares into quarters, yielding 52 squares 2½″ × 2½″ for the four-patches in both blocks.

- Trim 3 squares to 4½″ × 4½″ for the leaf stems.

From the red pile:

- Set aside 4 squares for the leaf HSTs.

- Cut 12 squares into quarters, yielding 48 squares 2½″ × 2½″ for the four-patches in both blocks.

- Trim 2 squares to 4½″ × 4½″ for the leaf stems.

From the remaining 5″ precut squares:

- Cut an assortment of 70 rectangles 4½″ × 2½″ for the scrappy pieced border.

- Cut 4 squares 2½″ × 2½″ for the pieced border cornerstones.

White solid

- Cut 2 strips 12½″ × WOF. Subcut into 30 rectangles 12½″ × 2½″ for the Four-Patch block.

- Cut 2 strips 8½″ × WOF. Subcut into 30 rectangles 8½″ × 2½″ for the Four-Patch block.

- Cut 4 strips 5″ × WOF. Subcut into 30 squares 5″ × 5 ″ for the leaf HSTs.

- Cut 2 strips 4½″ × WOF. Subcut into 15 squares 4½″ × 4½″ for the leaf block corners.

- Cut 2 strips 4½″ × WOF and 1 strip 2½″ × WOF. Subcut into 40 rectangles 4½″ × 2½″ for the Four-Patch block.

- Cut 3 strips 3¾″ × WOF. Subcut into 30 squares 3¾″ × 3¾″ for the leaf stems.

- Cut 15 strips 2½″ × WOF for the inner and outer borders.

Binding

- Cut 9 strips 2½″ × WOF.

TIP Get creative with this quilt—try mixing up the colors so each leaf is multicolored or each Four-Patch block is scrappy. You can also rotate the Leaf blocks so the leaves are going in different directions. For a more dramatic look, use a darker background instead of a white background.

Making the Leaf Block

All seams are ¼˝ unless otherwise noted. Follow the pressing arrows shown in the illustrations. Use fabrics in the same colorway to make 1 block.

Select squares for each block from the same color pile. For each block, you will need 12 assorted print 2½˝ squares, 4 print 5˝ squares, 1 print 4½˝ square, 4 white 5˝ squares, 2 white 3¾˝ squares, and 1 white 4½˝ square. Make 2 Leaf blocks each in yellow, brown, red, green, aqua, and gray; make 3 Leaf blocks in orange.

Making the HSTs

1. Pair 2 white 5˝ squares with 2 print 5˝ squares. Refer to Making Two Half-Square Triangles (page 15) for more information on the technique.

2. Square up the 4 HSTs to measure 4½˝.

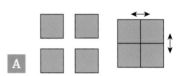

Making the Four-Patches

From the 12 squares 2½˝ × 2½˝ in assorted prints, assemble 3 four-patch units for the patchy part of the leaf, as shown. Press the seams open. FIG. A

Making the Leaf Stems

1. Use a 4½˝ stem square and 2 white 3¾˝ squares. Draw a diagonal line on the wrong side of the white squares.

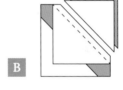

2. RST, position a white square on the bottom left and top right corners of the stem square. Sew on the diagonal lines. FIG. B

3. Trim ¼˝ away from the seam and press toward the white fabric to make a leaf stem unit. FIG. C

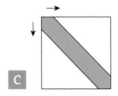

Assembling the Block

1. Layout the Leaf block, including 1 white 4½˝ square, 4 HSTs, 3 four-patch units, and the stem unit.

2. Sew the units together as a nine-patch, pressing the seams open. Repeat to make 15 Leaf blocks. FIG. D

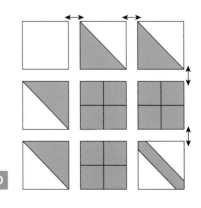

Making the Four-Patch Block

Make 2 yellow, brown, green, aqua, gray, and orange Four-Patch blocks and 3 red Four-Patch blocks.

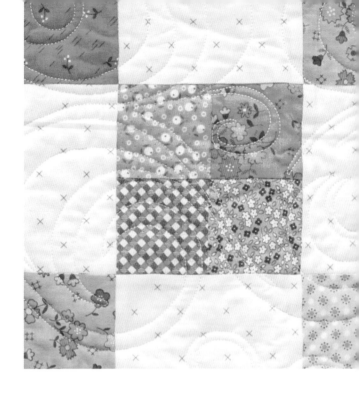

Making the Center Unit

Select 4 print squares 2½″ × 2½″ from one color pile. Sew together in a four-patch unit. Press seams open. This becomes the center unit.

Making the First Frame

1. Sew a white rectangle 4½″ × 2½″ to both sides of the four-patch center unit. Press toward the white fabric.

2. Choose 4 print squares 2½″ × 2½″ in a color different than the center unit to use as the corners. Sew a square to both ends of a white rectangle 4½″ × 2½″. Press toward the rectangle. Make 2 of these rectangle units.

3. Sew the rectangle units to the top and bottom of the four-patch unit. Press toward the rectangle units. FIG. E

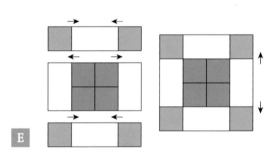

E

Making the Second Frame

1. Sew a white rectangle 8½″ × 2½″ to the sides of the block. Press toward the background.

2. Sew a 12½″ × 2½″ white rectangle to the top and bottom of the four-patch unit. Press toward the rectangle.

3. Repeat to make 15 Four-Patch blocks. FIG. F

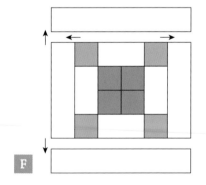

F

Pieced by Amanda Niederhauser, quilted by Kaylene Parry

Fabrics: Little Tree collection by Lella Boutique for Moda Fabrics + Supplies

cutting

Assorted black print fat quarters

- From each FQ, cut 4 strips 4″ × WOFQ. Subcut into 16 squares 4″ × 4″ for the star points. *Every 4 squares equals 1 set of star points.*

Assorted green print fat quarters

- From each FQ, cut 4 strips 2″ × WOFQ. Subcut into 16 rectangles 2″ × 3½″ for the block center frames. *Every 4 rectangles equals 1 frame set.*

Red fat quarter

- Cut 3 strips 3½″ × WOFQ. Subcut into 16 squares 3½″ × 3½″ for the block centers.

Gray solid

- Cut 4 strips 7¼″ × WOF. Subcut into 16 squares 7¼″ × 7¼″ for the Flying Geese.

- Cut 9 strips 2″ × WOF. Set aside 7 strips for the block four-patches. Subcut 2 strips into 25 squares 2″ × 2″ for the cornerstones.

White print

- Cut 2 strips 12½″ × WOF. Subcut into 40 rectangles 12½″ × 2″ for the sashing rectangles.

- Cut 11 strips 2″ × WOF. Set aside 7 strips for the block four-patches. Subcut 4 strips into 64 squares 2″ × 2″ for the block cornerstones.

Black floral

- Cut 8 strips 5″ × WOF.

Binding

- Cut 7 strips 2½″ × WOF; piece end to end.

Making the Star Block

All seams are ¼″ unless otherwise noted. Follow the pressing arrows shown in the illustrations.

Making the Block Center

1. To frame the center square, select 1 frame set. Sew a green rectangle to both sides of a red square. Press to the green rectangles.

2. Sew a 2″ white square to both ends of 2 green rectangles to make the final 2 frame units. Press toward the green fabric.

3. Complete the center-block frame by sewing a frame unit to the top and bottom of the red square unit. Press the seams toward the red square. Make 16 center units.

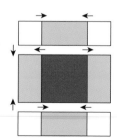

Making the Flying Geese Units

1. Draw a diagonal line on the wrong side of a set of 4″ black star points.

2. Align 2 marked star-point squares to opposite corners of a 7¼″ gray square, RST. The 2 drawn lines merge into 1 continuous line from corner to corner. Sew a scant ¼″ seam on both sides of the continuous line. FIG. A

3. Cut on the drawn line to make 2 dog-ear units. Press. FIG. B

4. Align 1 star-point square to the gray corner of a dog-ear unit. Note that the marked line sits between the dog-ears. Sew a scant ¼″ on each side of the drawn line. Cut apart on the line to make 2 Flying Geese units. Press toward the star points. Repeat with the second dog-ear unit for a total of 4 Flying Geese units. FIG. C

5. Square up each Flying Geese unit to 6½″ × 3½″.
FIG. D

6. Repeat Steps 1–5 to make 16 sets of 4 matching Flying Geese units.

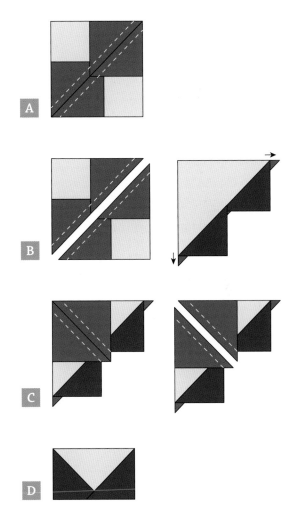

TIP Squaring up can be time consuming, but I've found that in the end it pays to have perfect Flying Geese. To ease the squaring-up process, use a small cutting mat that rotates 360°. You can even cut a 3½″ × 6½″ template out of heavy card stock to use as a guide for perfect Flying Geese.

Making the Four-Patches

1. Sew a white strip 2″ × WOF to a gray strip 2″ × WOF, RST lengthwise. Press the seams toward the gray fabric. Make 7 strip units.

TIP When pressing long lengths of seams like in the checkerboard construction, the seams can become curved. To avoid this, heat set the seam by pressing it flat first and then to one side. Also, make sure to use firm, direct pressure and not side-to-side ironing pressure. Give the seam a little tug to set it straight.

2. Cut the strip units in 2″ segments for 128 units total. FIG. E

3. Sew 2 segments RST, opposing the prints and matching the center seams to make a four-patch. Press to one side. Make 64 four-patches. FIG. F

Assembling the Block

1. Lay out the block using 4 four-patches, 1 set of 4 Flying Geese, and 1 center unit. Note the orientation of the four-patches in each corner.

2. Sew the block rows together. Press.

3. Sew the rows together. Press the seams open. Make 16 blocks. FIG. G

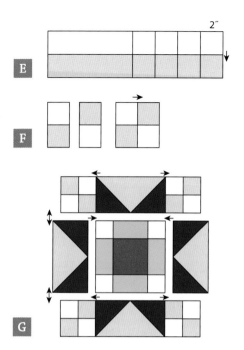

Assembling the Quilt

1. To make a sashing row, sew 5 gray cornerstones between and at each end of 4 white sashing rectangles. Press toward the sashing rectangles. Make 5 sashing rows.

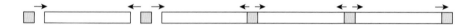

2. To make a block row, sew 5 white sashing rectangles between and at each end of 4 blocks. Press toward the sashing rectangles. Make 4 block rows.

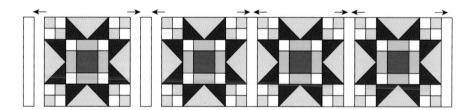

3. Beginning with a sashing row, sew the quilt together, alternating sashing rows and block rows. Press toward the sashing rows.

4. Piece the 8 border strips together end to end. Press the seams open. Subcut into 2 side borders 5″ × 56″ and 2 top and bottom borders 5″ × 65″.

5. Sew the side borders to the quilt front. Press toward the border. Sew the top and bottom borders to the quilt front. Press toward the border.

Finishing

For more details, see Finishing (page 16).

1. Baste the quilt backing, batting, and quilt top together. Hand or machine quilt as desired. This quilt was machine quilted with a snowflake swirl design.

2. Make the binding and attach it to the quilt.

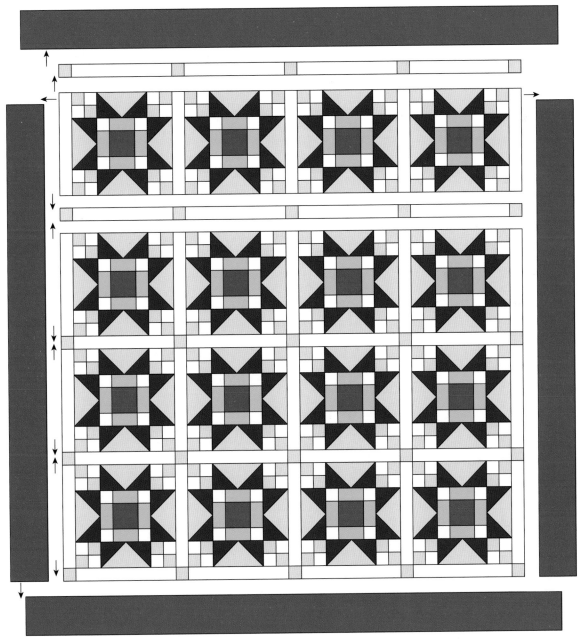

Quilt assembly

one-block wallhanging

Small quilts are my favorite! I have them all over my house: on tables, on walls, and tucked in baskets. Small quilts are quick to make and perfect for gift giving. Choose any block from this book and pop it into the quilt setting. You can customize it for any holiday or occasion. Use your fabric stash for a scrappy feel!

The fabric requirements, cutting measurements, and construction instructions are for the quilt setting only. Refer to the Scrappy Hearts block (page 40) or any of the center blocks for the fabric requirements and instructions for the 12″ center block.

materials

Materials listed are for the background, borders, backing, and binding only.

5″ PRECUT SQUARES:

  8 assorted reds

  4 assorted prints *each* in green, yellow, blue, and teal

WHITE SOLID: ½ yard for background

BINDING: ¼ yard

BACKING: ⅞ yard

BATTING: 30″ × 30″

Pieced and quilted by Amanda Niederhauser
Fabrics: A selection of 30s reproduction prints

5″ precut squares

- Trim the red, green, yellow, and blue squares to measure 4″ × 4″.

- Cut the teal squares to measure 3½″ × 3½″.

White solid

- Cut 2 strips 4″ × WOF. Subcut into 12 squares 4″ × 4″.

- Cut 1 strip 3½″ × WOF and use 1 scrap. Subcut into 12 squares 3½″ × 3½″.

Binding

- Cut 3 strips 2½″ × WOF.

Making the Wallhanging

All seams are ¼″ unless otherwise noted. Follow the pressing arrows shown in the illustrations.

1. Make any of the 12″ center blocks featured in this book for the center of this wallhanging. Press all seams open.

2. To make 32 HSTs, match up the 4″ white and print squares into pairs. Refer to Making Two Half-Square Triangles (page 15) for more information on the technique. These are the 16 pairs needed:

- 2 pairs of yellow and white
- 2 pairs of yellow and blue
- 2 pairs of green and white
- 2 pairs of green and blue
- 8 pairs of red and white

3. Square each HST to measure 3½″ × 3½″.

4. Arrange the HSTs and the white and teal squares around the center block, as shown.

5. Sew the squares and HSTs together in each of the top 2 rows. Press. Sew the top rows together.

6. Repeat Step 5 for the bottom 2 rows. Press.

7. Sew the side HSTs together as pairs. Press. Sew the pairs together to make 2 side columns.

8. Sew the columns sides to the 12″ center block. Press.

9. Sew the top and bottom rows to the quilt. Press.

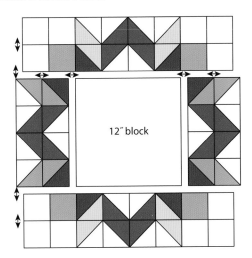

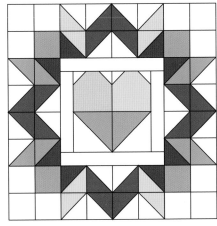

Quilt assembly

Finishing

For more details, see Finishing (page 16).

1. Baste the quilt backing, batting, and quilt top together. Hand or machine quilt as desired. This quilt was machine quilted with a loopy design.

2. Make the binding and attach it to the quilt.

Inspiration

Here are a few examples of different blocks in the center of the quilt. Get creative and have fun!

three-block table runner

I love decorating my house for each new season. I change my pillows, wall quilts, and table quilts almost every month. I love sewing table runners because I can use my fabric stash, they sew up quickly, and they are fun to give as gifts. This table runner features three blocks measuring 12″ square, set with pinwheels and sashing strips. You can mix and match any three blocks from this book! Use the block from *Leaf Peeping* (page 84) for a fall runner, from *Cozy Farmhouse* (page 92) for a Christmas runner, or from *Summer Picnic* (page 78) for a summer runner.

The block in this sample quilt is from *Rise and Shine* (page 28). Use your favorite color combination to make a table runner suitable for any occasion!

The fabric requirements, cutting measurements, and construction instructions are for the quilt setting only. Refer to the Rise and Shine block (page 28) or any of the center blocks for the fabric requirements and instructions for the 12″ center block.

materials

Materials listed are for the sashing, backing, and binding only.

PINK: ⅛ yard for pinwheels

WHITE SOLID: ½ yard for background

PINK-AND-WHITE FLORAL: ¼ yard for border

BINDING: ⅓ yard

BACKING: 1½ yards

BATTING: 54″ × 24″

Pieced and quilted by Amanda Niederhauser

Fabrics: Posy Garden collection by Carina Gardner for Riley Blake Designs

cutting

Pink

- Cut 1 strip 2½″ × WOF. Subcut into 16 squares 2½″ × 2½″ for the pinwheels.

White solid

- Cut 1 strip 3½″ × WOF. Subcut into 2 rectangles 3½″ × 12½″ for the sashing.

- Cut 1 strip 2½″ × WOF. Subcut into 16 squares 2½″ × 2½″ for the pinwheels.

- Cut 3 strips 2″ × WOF for the border.

Pink-and-white floral

- Cut 3 strips 2″ × WOF for the border.

Binding

- Cut 4 strips 2½″ × WOF.

Making the Table Runner

Make any 3 of the 12″ center blocks featured in this book. Press all seams open.

Making the Pinwheels

1. Pair 16 white 2½″ squares with 16 pink 2½″ pinwheel squares to make 32 HSTs. Refer to Making Two Half-Square Triangles (page 15) for more information on the technique.

2. Square up each HST to measure 2″.

3. Assemble the pinwheels by sewing 4 HSTs together in a four-patch, as shown. Make 8 pinwheels.

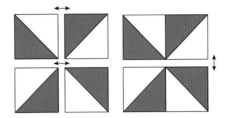

Making the Pieced Border

1. Make a strip set by sewing a 2″ white strip to a 2″ floral strip lengthwise. Press. Make 3 strip sets.

2. Subcut the strip sets into 8 border segments 12½″ × 3½″.

3. Make the pieced border by sewing 4 pinwheel blocks between and at each end of 3 border segments, as shown. Make 2 pieced borders.

Assembling the Table Runner

1. Sew 2 white 3½″ × 12½″ sashing rectangles between the 3 center blocks. Sew the 2 remaining border segments to each end of the block row. Press.

2. Sew the pieced borders to the top and bottom of the block row.

Finishing

For more details, see Finishing (page 16).

1. Baste the quilt backing, batting, and quilt top together. Hand or machine quilt as desired. This table runner was machine quilted with a floral design.

2. Make the binding and attach it to the quilt.

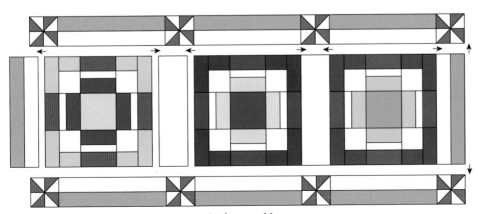

Quilt assembly

four-block quilt

Quilting can be a meaningful way to express love, congratulations, or sympathy for someone. This four–block quilt is a nice size to give as a baby quilt, a lap quilt, or a wallhanging. Simply choose any four blocks for the center and follow the instructions for the borders. The combinations are endless! The blocks in this sample quilt are from *Garden Cat* (page 22), *Flower Basket* (page 74), and *Gingham Patches* (page 54).

The fabric requirements, cutting measurements, and construction instructions are for the quilt setting only.

materials

Materials listed are for the borders, backing, binding only.

LOW-VOLUME FLORAL: ¼ yard for HSTs

RED PRINT: ¼ yard for HSTs

NAVY FLORAL: ⅔ yard for outer border

AQUA: 4 squares 3½″ × 3½″ for cornerstones

BINDING: ½ yard

BACKING: 1¼ yards

BATTING: 44″ × 44″

Pieced and quilted by
Amanda Niederhauser

Fabrics: An assortment
from Bonnie & Camille
for Moda Fabrics + Supplies

Low-volume floral

• Cut 2 strips 4″ × WOF. Subcut into 16 squares 4″ × 4″.

Red print

• Cut 2 strips 4″ × WOF. Subcut into 16 squares 4″ × 4″.

Navy floral

• Cut 4 strips 4½″ × WOF. Subcut into 2 side borders 4½″ × 30½″ and 2 top and bottom borders 4½″ × 38½″.

Binding

• Cut 5 strips 2½″ × WOF.

Making the Pieced Border

All seams are ¼″ unless otherwise noted. Follow the pressing arrows shown in the illustrations.

1. To make 32 HSTs, pair 16 low-volume floral squares with 16 red squares. Refer to Making Two Half-Square Triangles (page 15) for more information on the technique.

2. Square up each HST to measure 3½″.

3. To make a pieced border, sew 8 HSTs together in a row, as shown. Press open. Make 4.

4. Add an aqua square to both ends of 2 pieced borders to make the top and bottom pieced borders.

Assembling the Quilt

1. Make any 4 blocks 12″ × 12″ and sew them together in a four-patch. Press.

2. Sew the pieced side borders to the quilt front.

3. Sew the pieced top and bottom borders to the quilt front.

4. Sew the navy floral side borders to the quilt front. Press toward the outer borders.

5. Sew the navy floral top and bottom borders to the quilt front. Press toward the outer borders.

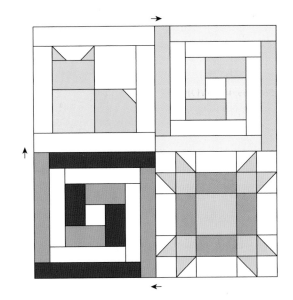

Finishing

For more details, see Finishing (page 16).

1. Baste the quilt backing, batting, and quilt top together. Hand or machine quilt as desired. This quilt was machine quilted with a swirl design.

2. Make the binding and attach it to the quilt.

Quilt assembly

About the Author

Amanda Niederhauser grew up at the side of her mother's sewing machine, playing with buttons, spools, and zippers. As a child and teenager she sewed pillows, shorts, scrunchies, and stuffed cats. It wasn't until she graduated college and moved to Virginia that quilting became her first love.

It was through trial and error that she taught herself to quilt, relying on books for information. She often tried to recreate quilts she saw in books and stores because there was no Etsy, Instagram, or internet from which to purchase quilt patterns. This early training of making her own quilt patterns helped her develop a love for quilt design and pattern making. Always inspired by fabric, she designs quilts for magazines, her blog, and her Etsy shop.

Most days, Amanda can be found at her Southern California home in her sewing studio with her cat, Mufasa. Amanda has an extremely patient husband, David, and three adorable children, Ella, Ryan, and Sally.

Photo by Nickell Photography

Visit Amanda online and follow on social media!

Website: jedicraftgirl.com

Pinterest: /aniederhauser

Facebook: /jedicraftgirlblog

Instagram: @jedicraftgirl

About the Author's Cat

Meet Mufasa, Amanda's trusty quilt assistant, the head of quality control, and the keeper of the fabric. Mufasa can be found in the sewing studio sleeping in baskets of fabric, sprawling on the cutting table, or batting at thread. He puts his paw print of approval on every project.

Photo by Amanda Niederhauser